purestyle

Jane Cumberbatch
photography by **Henry Bourne**

RYLAND
PETERS
& SMALL
LONDON NEW YORK

For this edition
Designer **Sarah Fraser**
Editor **Miriam Hyslop**
Picture Research **Tracy Ogino**
Production Manager **Patricia Harrington**
Art Director **Gabriella Le Grazie**
Publishing Director **Alison Starling**

First published in
the United Kingdom in 1996,
this edition first published in 2005 by
Ryland Peters & Small
20–21 Jockey's Fields
London WC1R 4BW
www.rylandpeters.com

10 9 8 7 6 5 4 3 2

Printed and bound in China.

ISBN 1 84172 864 0

A CIP record for this book is available
from the British Library.

contents

introduction

Pure Style is not just about rooms and furnishings, or about trying to achieve an impossibly perfect glossy lifestyle – *Pure Style* is about trying to achieve a balance. It's about making life luxurious, not in a costly, glitzy sense, but in a more matter-of-fact, practical and natural way. *Pure Style* is about paring down and trying to live with less clutter (the fewer things we have to fuss about, the more we can get on with living). It's about simple, basic design that combines function and beauty of form – crisp, clean, classic and timeless.

Pure Style: *innovative ideas for crisp, clean, contemporary living.*

pure style

Pure Style is about being economical but without skimping on essential things like good food or a decent bed. *Pure Style* is not all about slavishly following fashions in interiors, it's about being practical and resourceful – tracking down great domestic staples that have been around forever, using the high street chain stores for good basic buys, or seeking out second-hand furniture that can be revitalized with a lick of paint. *Pure Style* focuses on the sensual side of living: such as texture – frothing soap, rough log baskets, string bags, a twiggy wreath entwined with fresh rosemary sprigs, or the bliss of sleeping in pure white cotton sheets; smell – fresh flowers, sweetly scented candles or laundry aired outside in hot sun; tastes – good bread or new potatoes cooked with fresh mint; colour – light, bright, airy, matt shades inspired by nature, cow parsley, egg and calico whites, butter and straw yellows, bean greens, sea and sky blues, and earth tones; natural things – moss, lichen, shells, pebbles; scents – great coffee, chocolate and delicious wine; fabrics – good value, durable and decorative, in simple patterns like checks and stripes; basics – functional items that look good, such as a tin mug, a pudding basin or glass Kilner jars. *Pure Style* is about creating living, breathing spaces throughout the house. The book shows you how to be functional and practical in the kitchen, with durable work surfaces, proper cupboards and essential kitchen kit. *Pure Style* is about making the rituals of eating as sensual as is practicable or possible and shows you how simple ideas – white plates, starched linen and jars of cut flowers – can create pleasing and visually satisfying arrangements. *Pure Style* also demonstrates how plain but delicious basic ingredients – good cheese, fresh fish, fresh fruit and vegetables – are the key to hassle-free food preparation. In the sitting room, *Pure Style* illustrates how a combination of elements and textures, such as comfortable seating, beautiful fabrics in cotton, wool and muslin, and candlelight and blazing fires, help to make living rooms relaxing and peaceful. To help you slumber more soundly, *Pure Style* shows you the benefits of well-made beds and proper mattresses as well as the luscious qualities of crisp cotton bedlinen, snuggly warm woollen blankets and quilts. In the bathroom, the book demonstrates how access to plenty of piping hot water, together with soft cotton towels and wonderful scented soaps, can make bathing a truly sybaritic experience.

 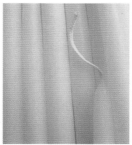 

elements

To touch, to hold, to look, to smell, to taste: the sensual aspects of life are there to be nurtured and encouraged. Engage the senses and explore the visceral elements around you. Douse your sensibilities with tactile elements; encourage and incorporate colour and texture into your home to make life an altogether more spirited and rewarding affair.

colour

Use colour to make daily living more pleasurable, spirited and uplifting. Thinking about how colour appears in nature gives clues to choosing the sorts of colours you might want to have in your home. Neutrals are timeless and easy to live with, while white is unifying, restful and a favourite with those who seek a simple approach to living. Greens are versatile, ranging from the brightest lime to much sludgier tones, and earthy hues of brown can be used for a variety of looks. The sea and sky colours found in denim, on china, bedlinen and in paint give clarity and crispness to interior settings. Look at garden borders to appreciate the range of pinks and transfer these indoors as soft lilac walls or muted floral cottons. Creams and yellows are cheerful, optimistic colours and have universal appeal. *Pure Style* is not about slavishly coordinated colour schemes, although it does show you how to put together rooms and interiors with accents on colour. It is more about considering the colours of everything around and incorporating them in our daily lives. Colour is a vital element in characterizing an interior and it need not be expensive. If you can't afford a complete redecoration, subtly change the emphasis with different cushions, covers and splashes of floral detail.

whites

Milk

Egg white

Wax white

Bone

Oatmeal

Calico

Brilliant white, eggshell white, bone white, lime white, even plain old white, all come in a plethora of contrasting hues and tones. White creates a peaceful and timeless ambience which benefits both period, and starker contemporary settings equally. It is a minimalist's dream shade and makes for harmonious, unifying spaces. In today's super-charged, techno world it's good for the soul to retreat into a reviving white oasis where simplicity rules. For an all-white scheme, strip then paint floorboards in white floor paint and seal with a yacht varnish; use white emulsion on the walls and ceilings. So that the whole interior does not finish up looking too much like the inside of an icebox, create toning contrasts by giving the woodwork touches of off-white, bone, or white with grey. For a unifying effect paint furniture in similar shades and add cotton drill slip-on covers, calico cushions and filmy muslin drapes. Complete with accessories such as white china and bedlinen, available from big department stores at bargain prices during the sales.

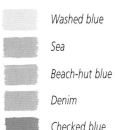

Washed blue

Sea

Beach-hut blue

Denim

Checked blue

blues

Blue spans a host of colour variations, from deep hyacinth to very pale ice. Blue can turn to lavender when mixed with violet, and turquoise when blended with green. In the middle of the spectrum are the purer blues of cornflower and bright powder blue. Take a cue from the fashion world and look at the soft blues that characterize denim as it is washed and worn. These shades adapt as easily to home furnishings as they do to jeans and jackets. Pale shades are the tones most likely to appear cold, especially in north-facing rooms. The trick here is to use warming devices, such as faded kelims or terracotta flower pots, perhaps in a room with duck-egg blue walls. If a pure blue is too strong for your taste then try a more sludgy mix of grey, green and blue – this works well with highlights of white; or try a dining room scheme in a sludge-blue, offset with white-painted furniture, curtains in blue-and-white check and bowls of white narcissi. For a more homespun look, combine the muted Shaker blues with red-and-white striped or checked cotton.

Useful decorating details in blue include tartan china and clear glass. There is blue-and-white striped ticking for loose covers and storage bags. And for a jaunty beach-house theme, make chair covers in bright lavender-blue cricket stripe cotton, together with faded blue-jean cotton cushions (various denim weights are available from fabric wholesalers).

Leek

Spring green

Pea

Herb

Cabbage

Garden

green

Green is one of the most accommodating colours for interiors. In a contemporary setting a vivid apple green or lime teamed with flourishes of fuchsia pink can work well, while traditional interiors call for duller shades mixed with grey, such as hopsack and olive. Take inspiration from the range of greens in nature; look at the bright lime-green stems of hyacinths or blades of fresh spring grass. Peas in their pods and cabbage leaves provide another

source of vibrant and sometimes variegated greens. Try using sage-and-white striped cotton for chair covers with bursts of lime-green for cushions.

pink and lavender

Pink needn't be the sickly colour we associate with frilly, little-girl bedrooms, over-the-top chintzy floral drawing rooms, or the monotonous peach-coloured bathrooms that are perennial in mass-produced home design catalogues. At the other extreme, shocking pink walls and ceilings are hardly a recipe for subtle, understated living. Careful selection and combining of pinks with other colours is therefore the key to making a stylish, comfortable statement. In contemporary settings fuchsia pink, lavender and green combine well – just look to the garden border for inspiration and think of purply lavender heads on sage-green foliage or foxglove bells with bright-green stalks and leaves. For a smart, up-to-the-minute scheme for a sitting room paint the walls white, cover chairs and sofas in pale lavender and make up cushions in plain fuchsia and lime-green cottons. Hot pink floral prints look great married with white walls and loose covers, creating a fresh, crisp and simple look. More delicate pink schemes need careful consideration to avoid looking bland. For a pink, though not at all prissy bedroom, paint the walls a warm shade such as a pale rose with a hint of brown

Hyacinth

Foxglove

Lavender

Marshmallow

Lilac

and furnish with an antique lavender-coloured patchwork quilt and calico Roman blinds – the whole effect will be clean and subtle.

On the edible front, think of enticing deep pink fresh strawberry ice cream; sticky and spongy marshmallows and violet cream chocolates. Less threatening to body shape are pink turnips, rhubarb, bitter radicchio leaves, and even pink pasta. For bright culinary detail try pink plastic textures, from mugs and brushes to buckets.

earth and terracotta

Because earthy hues are universally adaptable base colours it is hard to go wrong with them, except for those really drab mud-coloured schemes that were so popular during the seventies. Ranging from dark chocolate to cream, brown accents work in rustic and contemporary settings equally well. Consider the terracotta-coloured façades prevalent throughout Provençe and Spain, the brown woodwork and detailing of an English cottage kitchen, or the terracotta flags and wood beams in a New England farmhouse. In contrast imagine a white, utilitarian urban loft with dark wood schoolhouse-style desks, tables, chairs and filing cabinets. Study the shades of soil, from a clay-based red to a rich dark brown, and see how they act as a foil for brighter colours in nature. Clay pots are perfect for setting off the foliage and flowers of emerging spring bulbs. Be bold with earthy tones; for instance paint a dining room in a rich Etruscan shade for a warm effect both night and day.

Even boring beige is still a favourite shade and fabric companies love it for its versatility. Beige looks smart in various clever contemporary reworkings such as coir and natural fibre matting for floors, tough neutral linen for curtains and chair covers, or brown office files and filing boxes. Use striped and checked cotton in pinkish terracotta and white to make up chair covers and curtains with a wonderful natural feel.

 Chocolate

 Sack

 Coir

 Clay

Brick

yellow

Creamy country yellows are wonderfully adaptable and open up the meanest and darkest rooms to increase a sense of space. When decorating, opt for the softer end of the yellow spectrum as acidic yellows are harder to live with because of their sharpness. However, don't go too pale, as at the other

end of the scale very clear, light primrose shades can appear insipid. Creams and yellows look great with white, or even orange. Some shades look quite brown in the pot, but once on the walls are wonderfully rich and very well-suited to period hallways and kitchens. A slightly more acidic yellow will be lighter yet still rich in colour and should look good in artificial light and really glowing when the sun shines. There are also some very rich, bright yellows available and if you can stomach their intensity these gutsy shades illuminate and cheer up even the pokiest spaces, and look fabulous against blue-and-white china and furnishings. Cream or yellow looks good as paint on walls and as a decorative colour for furniture.

In a creamy kitchen, choose traditional stoneware pudding basins and white crockery to suit the simple theme. In living rooms, yellow walls look good against mustard-coloured check and plain cottons, with contrasting details in terracotta or blue. Yellows really come into their own in spring, when rooms are filled with daffodils and other spring flowers.

Butter

Honey

Pudding basin

Straw

Mustard

texture

Scant attention is paid to our senses by the purveyors of today's technological gadgetry with their ever-increasing obsession for convenience and labour-saving devices. There is not much textural appeal, for example, about computer hardware, or mass-produced, static-inducing synthetic carpets and fabrics. In complete contrast, sensual textures like soft, wool blankets, crisp cotton bedlinen and light and downy pillows are the domestic staples handed down from past generations that help to bolster us against the more soulless elements of modern living. From the perfect smoothness of a baby's skin to the gnarled and ridged bark on a tree, natural textures are there for us to take notice of and appreciate. They often combine an alluring mix of qualities. For instance, lumps of volcanic pumice stone, logs and shells are defined as rough or smooth, depending on the degree of erosion upon them by wind, sun, fire and rain. It is this very naturalness that compels us to gather such things about the house. Our homes need natural textures to transform them into living, breathing spaces – and polished wooden floors, rough log baskets, and pure cotton fabrics are just some of the organic ideas we can introduce to suggest this effect.

smooth

Smooth things are often fresh, clean things and appear all round the house, especially in the kitchen and bathroom. Washing activities spring to mind, such as a handful of frothing soap, or a big plastic bucketful of hot soapy water. Satisfyingly smooth surfaces of crisp white tiling, marble or utilitarian stainless steel conjure up a sense of clinical, streamlined efficiency. In kitchens, culinary preparation is made more efficient and hygienic when work surfaces can simply be sluiced, wiped down and made pristine. Utensils such as sparkling stainless steel pots and pans also help to keep culinary operations running smoothly. I love to cook with a selection of worn wooden spoons which have somehow moulded to my grip after years of devoted use. Smooth, cast-iron bath surfaces and ceramic tiled walls can be scoured and scrubbed, so helping to keep bathrooms squeaky clean. Indoors as well as out, natural surfaces such as slate or well-worn flags are texturally pleasing. Smooth elements exist in a diversity of guises, from crisp white tissue paper tied up with silk ribbon to polished floorboards. On a food theme, goodies include the wonderful slippery-smooth waxed paper

that serious shops wrap cheese in, slender glass
bottles of olive oil, or slivers of fine chocolate in
layers of the thinnest silver paper. You can also
bring naturally smooth objects, such as ancient
weathered pebbles and scoured driftwood
collected on an impromptu beach hunt, indoors
for textural decoration.

rough

One of my favourite possessions is a roughly hewn olive
wood basket from Spain. Made from the winter prunings of
olive trees it is silvery-grey in colour, robust in design and a
sheer pleasure to touch and hold. The locals in Spain use
such baskets to transport eggs and wild mushrooms,
oranges or tomatoes from their vegetable patches – while
mine in London is filled with kindling for the fire. Rough,
tough and hairy flooring in sisal and coir is durable and
even when woven into patterns it still looks like a simple
texture. Equally, a rough terracotta tiled floor is not only
satisfying to walk on but if it is not laid in exact uniformity
it has the appearance of having been in place forever.
Rough textures in nature have usually been created
by the elements, and even sun-blistered paint, a painter
and decorator's nightmare, can create a visually pleasing

finish on a weathered old outbuilding. This sense of roughness allied to age means that unevenly plastered or distemper-covered walls, or features such as reclaimed battered tongue-and-groove panelled doors, can make even a new house look rustic. Rough can mean contemporary too, and utilitarian concrete walls and floors are common features in industrial buildings converted to open, loft-style living spaces.

Roughness isn't always a pleasing texture, as anyone with chapped hands or prickly wool next to the skin knows, yet some fabrics such as cotton towels worn rough by repeated washing are perfect for an exhilarating rub down after a shower. And tools such as pumice stones and hard bristle brushes assist exfoliation and improve circulation.

scent and taste

Scents and tastes are so evocative that childhood memories may be unexpectedly recollected with a certain waft of perfume or the aroma of a particular food. As a small girl on holiday in provincial hotels I invariably associated France with a cocktail of scents that included furniture polish, smelly plumbing and cooked garlic. In the same way, the first sweet grass cuttings of spring, evident as I pass by a newly mown field, park or suburban back garden, transport me back to games played on the lawn at my grand-mother's house in Devon. Smells quicken our senses, increase anticipation and act as powerful stimuli – there is nothing like the whiff of strong coffee and toast to entice slothful risers out of bed. Taste is crucial to the pleasure we take in eating. Fresh ingredients are vital to making things taste good, together with a knowledge and appreciation of basic cooking skills. There is a world of difference between a home-made hamburger and the creations served up at fast-food outlets. Smell and taste are closely related, and one without the other would diminish the intensity of many edible experiences. Consider the first strawberry of summer; the heady flowery scent is a beguiling hint of the sweetness to come.

flavour and fragrance

It is invigorating to have good smells around the
house. I love paper-white narcissi whose flowers emit
the most delicious sweet smell. Scented candles and
bowls of pot pourri are other sources of floral scents.
In the kitchen scents and tastes come to the fore:
the fragrant citrus tang of grated lemon peel
accompanies the preparation of sauces and puddings
and the earthy scent of wild mushrooms being fried
rapidly in butter is any food lover's idea of heaven.
Simple tastes are often the most sublime. What
could be more enticing than a bowl of pasta mixed
with garlic and a little olive oil, or a good,
strong cheese? Herbs such as basil, rosemary,
thyme and dill smell delicious and help to
draw out the flavours of food.

fabrics

Setting taste and aesthetic considerations aside, criteria for choosing one type of furnishing fabric over another include the suitability of the weight and weave for a type of furnishing and the fabric's ability to withstand the effects of wear and tear. Furnishing cotton, linen, wool, silk, synthetic and mixed fibres exist in a wealth of colours, textures and weights and with a little effort it should be possible to find just about anything you want at a price you can afford. If you fall for a really expensive fabric bigger than your budget, invest in a small amount for a cushion or two instead. Otherwise it's worth hunting in the sales for the larger quantities needed for upholstery. For good value basics go to an old-fashioned haberdashers and track down companies who supply television, film, theatre and artist's trades. These are great places to find varied weights of calico like those used for toiles in the fashion business, or extra wide widths of canvas used as stage backdrops, and cheap rolls of muslin that are employed by designers for costumes and sets. One popular silk specialist I know of carries stocks of coloured silks, including the type used for parachutes. Over the next six pages you will find lots of examples of utility fabrics.

light

Lighter weight fabrics are brilliant for simple, floaty window treatments. Make decorative half curtains from voile or muslin (see 24 and 27) panels with cased headings. Thread them onto narrow rods and anchor them within the window frame. Other lightweight curtain ideas include unlined cotton (see 6, 7, 8) or linen (see 22) drops with tapes or ribbon loops at the top. Basic roller blinds in fine fabrics (see 9) look subtle and understated in a cream or white decoration scheme. Perfect for bedrooms and bathrooms are filmy transparent loose covers in voile (see 12) for chairs with pretty, curvy shapes. Soft Indian cotton in bright lime green (see 26) and other hot up-to-the-minute shades are great for making up colourful and inexpensive cushion covers. If you're in the mood, run up your own sheets, duvet covers and pillowcases in cotton sheeting (see 1), which comes in very wide widths. Covers should fit loosely around a duvet and have a generous opening secured with buttons, Velcro, or simple ties to make them easy to slip on and off. Printed cotton lawn dress fabric is also worth considering for sprigged floral pillow cases and cushion covers. Cotton sheeting is also a great staple for lightweight tablecloths and napkins.

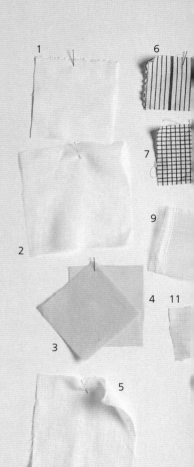

For details of the fabrics shown on pages 38–43 see pages 132–133

30

36

41

47

54

31

61

32

37

42

48

55

49

57

38

50

33

39

51

56

43

44

34

58

35

40

52

45

46

53

versatile

60

62

63

64

65   66

67

59

I have a passion for blue checked cotton (see 34 and 60) and use it all around the house for crisp colour and detail; as cushions (see 58 and 59) for assorted chairs and as Roman blinds (see 34 and 59) in the dining and sitting room. Blue checked loose covers also look good, and can be as basic or as decorative as you want – with bows, piping, ties or button detailing, simple pleats, short skirts or flowing hemlines. Window seat cushions in cream linen with a piped trim are smart, and this fabric also works well as an idea for covers on daybed bolster cushions. If the fabric is not shrink resistant, and covers are to be washed rather than dry-cleaned, pre-wash all materials including piping before making up. Blue-and-white striped ticking, a robust cotton twill closely woven in narrow stripes and traditionally used for pillows and mattress covers, is also another favourite (see 45) and looks especially good as simple curtains with ties at my attic windows, and across an alcove that houses children's clothes. Ticking is also a smart, classic idea for chair and sofa covers. Continuing on a striped theme, an all-time favourite is a lightish weight lavender-blue-and-white printed cotton (see 47) that I've used for tablecloths and cricket chair covers for summer suppers out in the garden.

durable

Tough all-purpose fabrics include canvas (see 82 and 83), sometimes known as duck, that is great for garden chairs and awnings. It's also good for Roman blinds and bolster covers. Creamy coloured calico is one of the best fabrics ever invented – it's incredibly cheap but manages to look smart and understated, and is durable, washable and perfectly practical. Calico comes in a number of weights; the finer qualities are more appropriate for loose covers or cushions, while thicker weights work well as blinds or curtains (see 75). Tough cotton denim (see 69) looks good on chairs after it's been put through several very hot washes to fade its dark indigo colour. For a crisp, tailored look chairs demand tight coverings to emphasize their shape. A self-patterned herby green cotton and viscose with simple tulips is one of my favourite upholstery fabrics (see 87), and it looks great on one of my secondhand armchairs. Sofas with a contemporary feel look wonderful in solid sea green and blue colours in tightly woven cottons (see 88, 89, 90). Alternatively, plain cream cotton is stylish, but choose some slightly more forgiving muddy-coloured linen if you have a family. Wool tartan (see 79) is another smart idea for upholstering the seats of dining chairs or sofas.

68 69 74
70
71 72 75
73

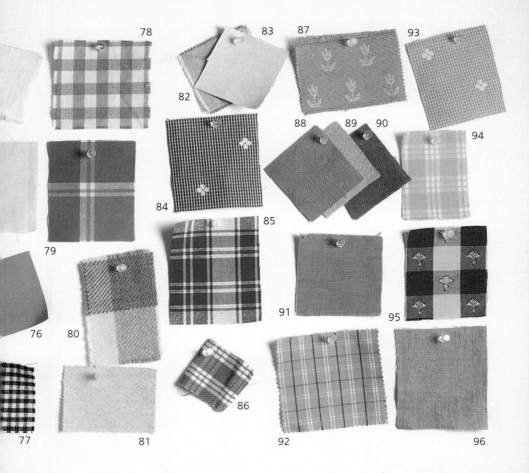

78

83

87

93

82

84

88 89 90

94

79

85

91

95

76

80

77

81

86

92

96

furniture

It may seem paradoxical, but I think that a diversity of objects can imbue an interior with a sense of character and uniformity. Old, new, decorative, industrial, contemporary or utilitarian, it's possible to combine a variety of furniture styles under one roof and yet create a strong visual statement. Fashion pundits and supermodels dictate the length of hemlines from season to season, but thankfully trends in interiors are less mercurial. But it is worth putting the same energies into assembling a look for your home as you would your wardrobe. As with desirable outfits, buy your furniture only after considering texture, comfort, shape and form. At home I have gathered together a hotchpotch of furniture from sales, second-hand shops and family – from 18th-century oak country dining chairs and old sofas to fold-up tables, painted junk sixties filing cabinets and kitchen chairs. My only proviso has been to weed out or revamp anything that I haven't liked the look of. Second-hand furniture designed for industrial and commercial use, such as swivel architect's chairs, bookcases from libraries and pattern-cutting tables from factories, can be re-invented happily in a domestic setting, and is better quality than mass-produced equivalents.

tables and chairs

I like chairs that have no frills or gimmicky details, in other words, chairs that look good, are robustly constructed and comfortable to sit on. Classic country chairs with rush seats are ideal for kitchens and dining rooms. Fold-up wooden slatted seats, the staples of church halls the world over, can be stowed away and are excellent for use in small spaces.

Like chairs, a table should look good, be strong and a pleasure to sit at. A basic table top perched on trestles is probably one of the most useful and portable shapes which can be set up or collapsed instantly. Junk shops are always good sources of chairs and tables alike – take your pick and revamp battered examples with a coat of paint.

above Stackable contemporary seating with beech-ply frame and splayed metal legs, inspired by the fifties butterfly chair by Arne Jacobsen.

above Big, basic and in solid pine: a definitive kitchen shape that would suit all kinds of interiors.

right A crisp bright pink cotton loose cover and a lick of white paint have given a junk chair a new lease of life.

right Perfectly angled to support the sitter's back, this worn but elegant little factory chair is a good example of functional but stylish seating.

below Based on a fifties shape, a zinc-topped wooden table is a streamlined idea for a gleaming contemporary kitchen.

below You can see examples of this sixties-style weatherproof aluminium café chair in bars and cafés throughout Europe – a great idea for urban backyards and loft spaces.

below Essential folding shapes for indoors and out: a white slatted chair and a metal dining table.

below Customized with eggshell paint, this simple pine table would make a smart desk or sidetable anywhere in the house.

below A white lime paint effect is a resourceful device for sprucing up an old turn-of-the-century pine table like this one.

above A simple trestle table like this one in birchwood-ply has a multitude of uses, ranging from a work desk to an impromtu dining table.

below Sturdy shapes in solid wood: a rustic beech chair with rush seating and a classic beech stool.

right A fold-up slatted beech chair, ideal for stowing away in small spaces, and an old wooden church chair – excellent durable seating for kitchens and dining rooms.

beds

Beds should be chosen for both practical and visual considerations. To ensure many peaceful nights of slumber it is crucial at the outset of any bed-buying exercise to invest in a decent mattress, and a solid base or frame. If you have limited funds think about ways of revamping your existing bed. For instance, lovely bed linen and blankets can disguise even the ugliest of divan shapes.

below right A traditional cast iron bed frame suits all kinds of interiors.

below left A Shaker-inspired pine four-poster (an amazingly good value flat-pack) is painted in white eggshell for a smart understated finish.

above Spare in shape and detail, and perfectly functional, this superbly streamlined bed in Douglas fir is a minimalist's dream.

above A contemporary shape, excellent for sprawling out on.

right This romantic French daybed is good for tight spaces.

below A Swedish-style wooden sofa with check covers, and a generously proportioned armchair.

sofas and seating

Good springs and sound construction are essential for comfortable upholstered seating. It's worth buying a good second-hand sofa or armchair with a wooden frame and strong interior springs, stuffing and webbing, rather than something new and less sturdily put together. Cover sofas in tough upholstery weights of linen and wool, or devise loose covers which can be as basic as a throwover sheet, or opt for a tailored pull-on design in washable cotton.

furniture

49

this page Laminated drawers with wire baskets are a clever reincarnation for flat-pack kitchen units.

opposite, top right Remember school cloakrooms? This metal mesh wardrobe is great for small spaces.

opposite below, left to right A decorative wooden dresser or visellier like this looks at home in country settings; bought cheaply from a second-hand shop, this simple chest of drawers was improved by a coat of paint; a walk-in wardrobe is one of the most effective ways of stowing away everything from clothes to suitcases.

cupboards and storage

In an ideal world storage should be devised to leave maximum living and breathing space. In reality we are hampered by budget, cramped rooms, too little time, too many occupants and too much clutter to set about the task of arranging ourselves a little more efficiently. Here are some ideas to make clearing away a more fruitful and inspiring exercise. Basic wooden shelving is one of the cheapest means of stowing everything from kitchen paraphernalia to bathroom towels, or scores of books. Free-standing storage notions include simple flat-pack systems – these are basic structures in pine that are good for utility rooms and children's rooms. If home is an attic flat with poor access, put together flat-pack cupboards or wardrobes on site.

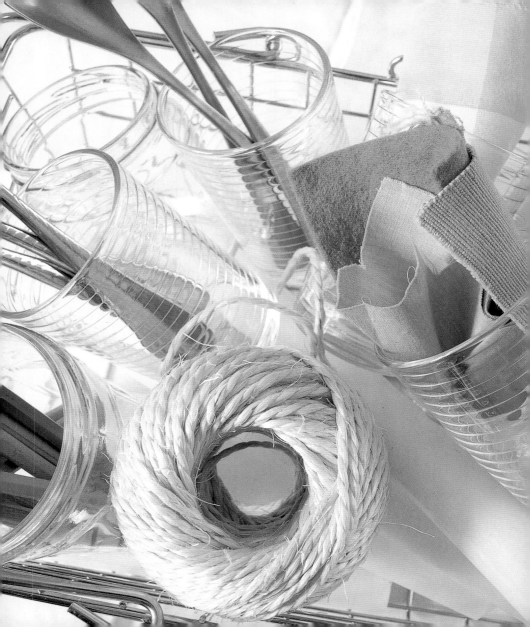

objects

If we all made inventories of our possessions how many things could we designate as being not really useful, or something we hate but can't give away because it was a present or a family heirloom? It might be painful for your conscience, but in the long run paring down unnecessary household clutter eases the path to a more practical and soothing existence. Don't be sentimental about hoarding items that you'll never use. Identify the things that give you pleasure to hold, to use and look at. It's more useful to have one really good saucepan rather than have three second-rate ones that burn everything you cook. Even something as basic and utilitarian as a slender wood and bristle broom is a thing of beauty and just as humbly aesthetic as the rough mesh structure of a metal sieve, or a good old-fashioned mixing bowl whose deep curvy proportions are perfectly evolved to perform its tasks. Do away with those dusty lampshade bases made from Chianti wine bottles that your mother gave you for your first flat. But resurrect classic anglepoise desk lights, as those in the know continue to appreciate their supple proportions. Vernacular objects so perfectly designed to fulfil their function are works of art in their own right.

utensils

Whenever I have to make do with a temporary or makeshift kitchen during house renovations the surrounding chaos is bearable so long as I've had access to water, something to cook on and a fridge. My survival kit of kitchen tools under such siege conditions includes a cast-iron enamelled cooking pot in which to conjure up everything from early-morning breakfast porridge to herby chicken casseroles, a sharp knife, a solid chopping board, a pile of wooden spoons, and, to keep spirits from flagging and the caffeine levels high, a metal stove-top espresso maker. Other crucial equipment includes scissors, a garlic crusher and, of course, a decent corkscrew.

Some of my favourite tools: a garlic crusher (that also stones olives), a balloon whisk and fish crackers, ideal for attacking crab.

What kitchen would be complete without a kettle? Invest in a sturdy and hard-wearing metal catering one for endless rounds of satisfying brew-ups.

A glass citrus fruit squeezer is a nifty tool for producing small amounts of orange, lemon, lime or grapefruit juice.

Produce mounds of crisp, crunchy vegetables that really keep their flavour, or poach small pieces of fish, with a heavy-bottomed stainless steel steamer.

A robust cast-iron enamelled casserole is excellent, whether you are cooking for a crowd of friends, a simple family meal or just for one or two.

Drain everything from pasta and rice to salad leaves with a simple metal colander, and borrow or buy a fish kettle to take the angst out of cooking large fish like salmon in one piece.

left Some basic metal tools: a sieve for sifting flour or draining vegetables and a boxy grater for demolishing hunks of cheese such as Parmesan.

left Wonderful to hold, and perfectly proportioned, a stainless steel frying pan for rustling up everything from risotto to fish steaks.

above Found in just about every continental kitchen, a classic stove-top espresso maker is an easy way to make steaming-hot strong coffee.

Life would be impossible without a really good sharp stainless steel knife, a pair of scissors and a corkscrew!

For fishy treats: a strong oyster knife with a protective guard, and classic cutlery with bone-handled knives.

objects

55

lighting

We can appreciate that daylight is the perfect light, because there is the dark with which to compare it. But night suffuses everything with its own particular mood and bestows its own impressions and textures. Without darkness we would be deprived of the luxury of candlelight which is the most sensual, calming and benign of all sources of light. Lit candles highlight a dark room with luminous flickering qualities that bring us in touch with the sensations of a pre-electric age. For a romantic dining room, invest in a simple metal or wooden chandelier and light it with candles. At its best, artificial lighting is subtle and effective. At its worst, the glaring horrors of naked light bulbs or the bland brightness of supermarkets speak for themselves. The most sensitive way to light interiors is with pools of subtle illumination, achieved with lamps set in designated corners, or with recessed low-voltage downlighters.

above and right For summer evenings, choose from curvy glass hurricane shades, lanterns and nightlights (easily found in hardware stores).

above right and opposite Utilitarian lamps and worklights look great in contemporary and more traditional settings alike. Overhead pendant lights in spun aluminium work well in kitchen and dining rooms, or as stylish hall lighting. For desk tops, anglepoise lights are not only smart but flexible practical gadgets that help illuminate all kinds of tasks.

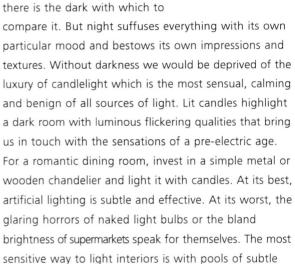

storage

Many small-scale storage ideas can be customized to look individual and imaginative. Reinvent old shoe boxes, for example, by covering them with fabric or paint to make colourful storage for your home office or for children's toys. Or use a lick of white paint to transform an ugly black clothes rail into a stylish moveable wardrobe, ideal for small living spaces; it can be covered with a white sheet to keep the dust off. I am an avid collector of old jam jars, and other domestic basics that double up as stylish containers include metal buckets (good for vegetables) and glass Kilner jars (they make even staples like rice, flour and pasta look good). Industrial meat hooks are available from good kitchen shops and are a great way to hang up your *batterie de cuisine*.

Empty jam jars with neat, good-looking proportions are ideal for accommodating anything from pens and pencils to flowers.

An ugly black clothes rail has been transformed by a lick of white paint into a stylish and moveable wardrobe, ideal for small living spaces. It can be covered with a white sheet to keep the dust off.

left A wooden two-tiered shoe rack, reminiscent of school cloakrooms, is useful for hallways and bedrooms.

left Display vegetables and other kitchen ingredients in classic aluminum buckets.

right Hang meat hooks from poles for instant hanging space. This old broom handle is supported by metal fittings.

left Empty wall space can be put to good use with a simple Shaker-style peg rack. These bags are made from washable cotton.

right Glass storage jars are both utilitarian and smart and can be filled with flour, sugar or pasta, or used for their original purpose, preserving.

below Recycle old shoe boxes and cover them with bright cotton fabric as an attractive storage solution in the office, or for children's toys.

left For a smart contemporary look stash spoons and cutlery in metal pots and arrange them in rows on shelves and kitchen surfaces, where they are handy for use.

right A junk shop basket is a useful solution for bulky items such as this thick checked blanket made in Wales and cushions covered in blue and green cotton.

objects

59

display

Making a statement about the way you display favourite things, from photographs to kitchen pots and pans, is all part of creating order and giving your living space a characteristic look. There is something arresting to the eye to see collections of basic vernacular objects – even something as common or garden as plain white mugs can look good *en masse*.

Use natural elements to devise beautifully simple display ideas such as collections of pebbles from the beach; shadow boxes filled with leaves, shells and china fragments from the shoreline; and collections of roughly hewn olive baskets.

left A favourite collection of old
pudding basins is arranged simply in
an old corner cupboard.

above Bowls or jars planted with
your favourite spring bulbs and simple
wood-framed shell prints look great
arranged in groups.

objects

61

china and glass

The quality, shape and size of what you drink out of or eat off is pivotal to really relishing what is in your glass or on your plate. I like the ribbed, chunky qualities of Duralex glasses which are robust and a pleasure to drink from. The classic proportions of plain white plates also make eating a really pleasing affair; food looks good on them too.

above Creamware china for refreshing brews, including a great big cup for warming milky breakfast coffees.

below Any self-respecting café dispenses strong black espresso coffee in little heavy-bottomed cups with saucers. Imbibing out of anything larger, or flimsier would diminish the experience.

right Blue-and-white spongeware: very decorative for informal settings, and it also looks good on dressers and shelves.

below Workaday glassware for knocking back iced water, slugs of sherry, bubbly and other thirst quenchers.

right Chunky white china mugs from just about any chainstore are essential kitchen kit.

A fabric design from north of the border: blue-and-white tartanware for serving up shortbread, oatcakes and other Scottish treats.

Blue-and-white striped china is bright, basic and comes in lots of versatile shapes. It's great for everyday use.

Jolly blue-and-white checked china is a cheery sight on the breakfast table. This shallow bowl is useful for dishing up cornflakes and other staples.

You can't beat plain blue-and-white bone china for simple and stylish kitchen schemes – one of my all-time favourites.

left Classic white bone china plates are my favourites, and make the humblest meal look really appetizing.

Perfectly formed bowl shapes – for serving everything from porridge and puddings to soups and salads.

right A classic jug shape – they come in lots of different sizes and they also make great vases for flowers.

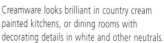

A choice of vessels for dedicated coffee drinkers: tiny chocolate brown cups for small shots of pure caffeine, like espresso, or a heavy-bottomed cup for capuccino.

Creamware looks brilliant in country cream painted kitchens, or dining rooms with decorating details in white and other neutrals.

putting it all together

Colour and comfort are key ingredients in putting rooms together. Bright, light, airy shades of white and cream create inviting spaces, as do stronger greens, lavenders and blues. Choose furniture that combines function with style, and stick to basic shapes. Think about texture to help bring life into your surroundings; draw from nature for inspiration.

culinary living

There are an awesome number of items that need to be squeezed into the average kitchen: boxes of breakfast cereals, pots, pans, dishwasher, fridge, sink – the list is endless. Storing and incorporating it all requires planning and thought. Cupboards, drawers, shelves and work surfaces should be considered both for functional and aesthetic appeal. Make surfaces durable and use basic materials like wood, marble, slate and stainless steel. Pare down your kitchen kit to the most basic essentials. Make the daily rituals of eating as pleasurable as is possible or practical. Eat off simple white plates, drink from good glasses, light candles, fill jars with flowers and spread a crisp white linen cloth for special occasions. Preparing food can be a therapeutic experience even if you are busy with work or family. Avoid food fashions (what is it this month – French, Italian or outer Mongolian?) and resist long-drawn-out recipes with impossible-to-find ingredients. Don't become a nervous wreck looking for exactly the right type of extra-virgin olive oil. Stick to food that you like and do well. It's far better to serve up an excellent cheese on toast than a second-rate and unremarkable attempt at something more flashy.

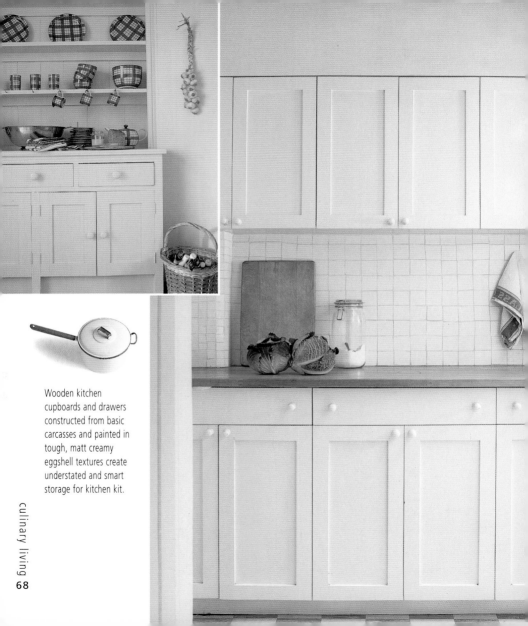

Wooden kitchen cupboards and drawers constructed from basic carcasses and painted in tough, matt creamy eggshell textures create understated and smart storage for kitchen kit.

In the past, kitchens were purely rooms in which to prepare and cook food, while dining rooms were set apart as separate rooms dedicated to eating. To meet the demands of late 20th-century living, kitchens have evolved as spaces which fulfil all sorts of functions, so that eating and living are frequently combined. Different settings dictate different priorities. Rural kitchens need to cope with the toing and froing of muddy feet or paws and are the natural habitats of wonderful warming stoves such as Agas and Rayburns, which are both practical and stylish machines.

In town, there is more emphasis on the clever siting of labour-saving devices such as dishwashers, electric juicers, microwaves and so on, to help deal with the pressures of city life.

Most food preparation takes place on durable surfaces and there are various options. Oiled regularly and kept pristine with frequent scrubbing, worktops in maple or beech are the ultimate luxury, albeit a costly one. A cheaper solution is to buy lengths of beech block from large DIY outlets. Salvage yards are also a good source of reclaimed timber for work surfaces, for example I found a bargain teak draining board from a Victorian almshouse at a country salvage yard. Despite its association with glossy Hollywood-style bathrooms, marble is a robust, hygienic material and unpolished matt grey, white or creamy textures make practical, understated work surfaces. Marble is particularly affordable at source, for instance in southern France, Spain and Italy. For a really cheap kitchen facelift, laminated plywood is available in lengths from builders' merchants and comes in lots of different colours. The sink is a crucial part of the kitchen work surface and chunky, deep white ceramic Belfast sinks are ideal and can be picked up quite easily second-hand.

culinary living

left A bright, cheerful kitchen with a utilitarian feel. Pride of place is given to a magnificent forties cooker that deals with cooking operations as efficiently as any contemporary model. Crisp blue-and-white checked lino floor tiles and a cotton tablecloth complete the homey, relaxed atmosphere.

right Open wooden shelving left in bare wood or painted in the same colour as the rest of the kitchen is a practical and decorative way to display china, kitchen tins and containers.

Storage solutions are key to creating a well-organized kitchen. At the most basic level simple, open shelves in pine are incredibly useful vehicles for housing plates, glasses, culinary herbs and just about any other kitchen paraphernalia. Collections of tins and boxes in interesting shapes and colours make an attractive display. Screw cup hooks to the underside of pine shelving and you have instant hanging space for mugs, ladles, sieves and whisks. Not everyone is keen to have their kitchen contents on view, so cupboard doors hung on a basic carcass are the perfect camouflage for larder contents or a repertoire of pots and pans.

Wall-to-wall units and cupboards are practical but some custom-made schemes with fancy trims and detailing can be fantastically expensive. For a more individual look – and if you are strapped for cash anyway – combine a minimum of built-in elements such as a sink, cooker and worktop in a unit, together with free-standing features such as a second-hand dresser base jazzed up with paint, or an old metal factory trolley which is ideal for wheeling plates and dishes around. Other useful storage notions include a wall-mounted wooden plate drainer, or a tall, free-standing larder cupboard, ideal for filing with heavy items like tins, groceries and china.

right Blue-and-white striped cotton roller towel, used for chair covers or for table runners as here, can be sourced from specialist companies who supply institutions.

left Crisp plain white cotton tablecloths work in any setting. A row of narcissi planted in big pudding bowls creates simple, colourful and scented decoration for parties and everyday use.

Eating and drinking, however humble and low-key an affair, should be revelled in and made the most of. As well as deciding what to eat at any particular meal, what to eat it off and what sort of mood you want to convey are of equal importance. At the end of a gruelling day with three children there are few frills at my table, but it's still worth lighting candles or finding some ironed linen napkins to create a sense of occasion. Table settings needn't be elaborate affairs. Pleasing textures and well-made glass, china and cutlery are the crucial elements. On a day-to-day basis you might settle for a crisp check cloth with a jar of garden flowers, basic white plates and simple glass tumblers. When friends come it's worth pushing the boat out and laying a crisp, white linen cloth and napkins, together with candles, your best bone-handled cutlery and wine glasses.

The sales are brilliant sources of discounted china and where I go to buy seconds of white Wedgwood bone china plates. Street markets and junk shops are useful for single pieces of antique glass. During a weekly hunt around my local market in London's East End, I pounced upon half a dozen late-Victorian heavy wine glasses, each one different, and use them to serve up everything from jellies to drinks.

Department stores are good for table linen, together with an ever-growing number of mail-order companies. Alternatively, you could make your own tablecloths and napkins from specially wide linen from fabric wholesalers, or run up fabric by the yard or metre. If you're really stuck, simply use a plain white sheet. And if you have a children's party to organize, buy plain white disposable paper cloths available from most chainstores.

One of the best things about assembling table settings is thinking of natural greenery and floral components for decoration. In the autumn, plates of nuts or leaves look striking and so do vases of branches studded with bright red berries. At Christmas time I spray apples with gold paint and put them in a big wooden bowl for decoration on the table, or hang them on string from a chandelier. I also scatter small branches of Christmas tree cuttings

Wooden dining chairs come in a variety of shapes. Don't worry if yours aren't all the same design: a mix of styles, sourced from second-hand and junk shops, can look just as good as a fully matching set.

culinary living

77

on the table and for some early seasonal colour and scent there are pots of flowering narcissi or hyacinths. In early spring I like to fill metal buckets with the bright green sticky buds of chestnut branches or pussy willow, but summer tables are the most fun to create: I pick nasturtiums and sweet peas from my back yard and bring home armfuls of cow parsley after a day out in the countryside. Even a few jugs of fresh herbs, like rosemary, thyme, lavender or parsley make basic but beautiful decorations. Sometimes we've rented a cottage in Cornwall and there the summer hedgerows are thick with leggy purple foxgloves which are stunning for table embellishments simply stuffed into tall, clear glass jars and vases.

On trips to Spain everyone eats outside in the evening sitting around trestle tables laid with grilled fish, meat, pasta, bread, wine and cheese. After the glut of wild spring blooms such as orchids, daisies, buttercups, campion and lilies, it's harder to find flowers during the months of summer drought. A useful source is the local village market where squat, dark-skinned ladies sell white tuberoses, a few stems of which produce a glorious intoxicating scent as night falls. Otherwise the table is decorated with vases of silvery-grey olive cuttings. We get the barbecue going and cook up everything from sardines to slivers of pepper.

opposite page Plain white china plates, bowls and cups look great against any colour scheme, and always make food look appealing, however humble your offering. Specialist catering shops can often yield good buys.

this page Soft lilac emulsion on the walls is a good foil for covers in calico and a plain white cloth. A lime green checked cotton curtain and single stems of purple anemones provide a colourful contrast in this fresh and inviting dining set-up for two.

Table embellishments can be simple yet striking:

left Topiary shapes work well in terracotta flower pots. Try a leggy myrtle standard, like the one shown here, or other shapes in box or bay.

right A pretty candelabra, a lucky find in a Roman market, looks especially lovely at night.

The seating arrangements of any dining area are dependent upon the space that's available. If it is limited, tables and chairs might need to be of the fold-up variety and stowed away when necessary. On the other hand, generously proportioned rooms can accommodate big wooden refectory tables, or oval and round shapes and deep comfortable seating. Don't worry about having sets of matching chairs as disparate shapes, especially junk wooden kitchen chairs, can look quite good together and if you want to create a sense of unity you can cover them in simple pull-on loose covers in calico, or some other durable and washable texture. (See page 75 for some colourful examples in blue-and-white striped roller-towel cotton.)

culinary living

right Low-backed wooden office chairs on wheels and a mahogany door laid on metal trestles are inventive ideas that are well suited to the wide-open contemporary living space in this converted London industrial building.

Choose a table to suit the style of the rest of the dining area. Rustic farmhouse shapes in wood look good almost anywhere and are practical and robust. Very contemporary streamlined models with zinc, stainless steel or laminated surfaces suit more modern settings.

If furniture classics are your penchant, look to early 20th-century designs, such as simple ladderback oak chairs and solid oak tables, or more recent classics such as the sensually moulded white bucket-shaped Tulip chairs from the 1950s, shown on page 81. Since most people prefer suites of brand new dining furniture, excursions to markets and probing among second-hand shops can yield fantastic buys at bargain prices. If you need to make extra table space for a party you can make a very basic dining table from a piece of board or even an old door laid over a pair of trestles; simply disguise the makeshift base in a plain white sheet.

far right and below Refectory style: a plain table and benches in solid Douglas fir pine are spare and minimal solutions for dining. Equally streamlined are the full-length limestone bench seating down one wall and the open fireplace.

culinary living

82

Other useful elements for dining areas include a side table or sideboard from which to serve food or to display flowers or lighting. It's always handy to have supplies of plates, bowls and glasses close at hand, either stored on open shelving or in cupboards.

One of the highlights of winter is to be able to enjoy an open fire. If you are lucky enough to possess a working fireplace, gather some logs and kindling (or be practical and have them delivered) and give your guests the luxury of a warming blaze. Candlelight is the best and most romantic light to eat by. I buy creamy coloured church candles from a candlemaker at a nearby Greek Orthodox Church. If you don't possess particularly nice candlesticks, stick the candles on plain white plates or leave them free-standing for subtle illumination.

far right Colourful treatments for dining rooms include the yellow, green and blue scheme shown here. Pale cream walls in eggshell create a plain backdrop for splashes of more vibrant colours such as blue-and-white checked cotton Roman blinds, sofa cushions in lime green and blue, and a simple metal chandelier in matt yellow emulsion. On the table, the plastic green checked cloth, available by the metre from department stores, is smart and practical for everyday use. Flowering spring bulbs, bought cheaply by the tray from a local market, and planted in painted flower pots, provide scent and sunny detail.

relaxed living

Even the most frenetic workaholics need time to sink into a comfortable chair, put their feet up and contemplate life. Living rooms are tailored to meet the demands of their occupants – families with small children require battle-proof chairs and fabrics, while single individuals with no danger of sabotage by sticky hands might make a sumptuous wall-to-wall white scheme their priority. But whatever your family status, gender or age, comfort and texture are the most important factors for rooms in which you want to wind down. Use colours that soothe and are light enhancing – such as soft creams or bone whites – and keep paint textures matt. Buy really solid comfortable upholstery, and proper feather-filled cushions. Be selective with the fabric textures that you use. Seek out tough linens in beautiful creams and naturals, or strong woven cottons in ticking, checked and striped designs. Experiment with bright plain colours – blues, greens, pinks and orange. Explore the variety of warm woollen fibres, for use as upholstery, soft throws or insulating curtains. Bring the room alive with natural elements: light scented candles or soak up the warmth of a blazing fire.

Sitting rooms should be comfortable and relaxed rooms where you can sprawl out on a sofa with a good book, listen to music, watch the box, or simply sit back and think. Colour, comfort, texture and warmth are important factors in putting together an agreeable, functional space.

From curtains to loose covers, fabric colours can change a room as much as the impact of paint.

far right French metal daybeds can be found in salesrooms and antique shops and look great with striped cotton ticking bolsters or plain white cushions or throws. Paint them white or leave them bare.

right Blue-and-white is fresh with decorative details like crisp striped cushions and scrunchy Roman blinds, faded floral loose covers, and lots of checked cotton accessories.

Don't worry about slavishly matching the cushion cover, to the curtain lining, to the tie on your favourite slip cover. It is much more interesting to try out similar but contrasting fabric shades. I remember a room I decorated to a spring theme where creamy yellow walls contrasted with bright green-and-white checked blinds, together with loose covers in a dark cabbage-leaf colour and cushions in a lime green and thin blue-and-white striped cotton. The overall effect was bright, sunny and easy to live with.

Sitting rooms must be comfortable and this relies partly on well-made, sturdy upholstery. It is far more satisfactory to invest in a good-quality second-hand sofa, say, than something brand new,

mass-produced and lightweight. I know an enterprising woman who sells everything from hand-me-down Knole sofas from stately homes to junk armchairs, all piled up in barns and outhouses in a farmhouse. If you invest in new upholstery test it out for comfort before buying: sit on it for ten minutes, bounce up and down on the seat (you should be able to feel the underlying support); lean back (you should not feel any springs protruding from the framework); lift it to test the weight of the framework (it should not be too lightweight).

Upholstery fabric should be hardwearing. Some of the best fabrics are linen and linen–cotton mixes. A few years ago I found some wonderful earthy coloured linen reduced at a fabric outlet, on sale at 15 per cent of the usual price. I bought up ten metres which was enough to cover a Victorian chesterfield. Despite heavy wear and tear from parties, children, dogs and cats it is still looking respectable, only of course I am now itching to find another bargain. Loose or slip covers are practical for cleaning and a budget way of updating sofas and chairs.

Blues, greens and greys are useful colour tools.

right Powder blue paintwork looks sharp against bold navy striped slip covers and cushions in assorted shades of blue cotton stripe. White brickwork walls and whitened parquet flooring emphasize the airy feel.

far left A painted grey skirting adds subtle definition to plain white walls in a light and fresh Provençal sitting room. Reclaimed terracotta tiles laid in an uneven pattern add to the vernacular effect.

above Warming not cold: rich blue-green emulsion paint makes a distinctive foil for white woodwork, a plain white dustsheet throw and polished wooden floorboards.

this page Splashes of terracotta act as warming detail in the cream sitting room of a London Georgian townhouse. Amongst furnishing and fabrics in blues, greens and yellows there is a kelim rug in faded earth and brick. Spread across the marble mantlepiece are old clay pots and a rosemary wreath. Other rich ingredients seen below include old wooden Spanish soup bowls filled with rag balls made of scraps of checked and striped cotton and an antique three-legged milking stool.

far right A fold-up butler's tray acts as a versatile display idea with a candlestick lamp and a jug of spring flowers.

Loose covers can be made up with various details such as pleated or simple box skirts, self ties at the corners, or a row of buttons or a bow at the back. If you want a really instant update, cover up an unattractive sofa, perhaps in rented accommodation, with a white sheet or a simple check cotton throw. This is also a good idea for giving upholstery a change for the summer.

You can create a wonderful room with a great colour scheme and lots of decorative ideas, but if it's cold, it's miserable. The ultimate in warmth and atmosphere is a blazing log fire – and woods such as chestnut and apple give off delicious smoky scents. Ecologically sound but second-best is smokeless coal. Not everybody has access to wood, or the inclination to lay and maintain a real fire, so flame-effect fires are worth considering. Although they don't throw out as much heat as a real fire and

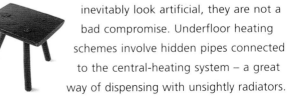

inevitably look artificial, they are not a bad compromise. Underfloor heating schemes involve hidden pipes connected to the central-heating system – a great way of dispensing with unsightly radiators.

this page Neutral tones of white and cream create a peaceful feeling with simple picture frames and streamlined lighting.

right Contemporary details include market finds such as a sixties basket chair and sunburst mirror.

far right Harking back to fifties gum commercials, the owner of this cosy panelled sitting room in a traditional shingled house on Long Island aptly describes the subtly coloured paintwork as chewing-gum grey. Rough sisal matting, pine planking (resourcefully salvaged from packing crates) and neutrally coloured linen fabrics add to the fresh and understated effect.

Cushions are important comfort factors. Buy proper feather or kapok-filled pads, as foam fillings are unsightly and lumpy. Pads squeezed into mean-sized covers don't look good, so make covers roomy and allow the cushion to 'breathe'. Simple piped cushions or flanged shapes are perennial classics. Bags with tie openings look good and are incredibly easy to run up on the sewing machine at home. You can make up cushions in just about any fabric – I like tough blue-and-white checked Indian cotton, striped ticking and light cotton in bright shades (which is good for a summery feel).

You can also recycle covers from chopped-up old curtains, table cloths and off-cuts of fabric in your favourite colours or patterns. Anything faded and floral, especially blues and whites or soft pinks and lavenders will work well with checks, stripes and plains. If, say, you hanker after a beautiful floral cotton but can't afford the hefty price tag for a big soft furnishing project, then why not buy just half a metre, the average price of a pair of shoes, and make it up into a beautiful cushion for a favourite chair. It will last considerably longer than the shoes!

right For a homespun feel with an updated edge this loft space has been decorated with pristine white walls, contemporary galvanized metal buckets and a primitive-style metal chandelier. Woven cotton bought in a sale has been used to make simple loose covers for a battered old sofa and chairs.

above More homespun ideas: disparate furniture from a sale is unified with soft grey paint.

Deep-pile, wall-to-wall white carpet might be appropriate in a boudoir-like bedroom, but for everyday stylish living natural flooring textures such as coir, sisal, seagrass and cotton, or wool rugs in checks and stripes, are more liveable with in terms of cost and practicality. For insulation, layer rugs over one another. Buy mats that are bound with hessian or woven cotton borders as these look better and prevent fraying. Cotton rugs are cheap and many are designed to be thrown in the washing machine, but remember that very bright colours might run and so should be carefully hand washed. Thick tartan wool rugs are a good investment.

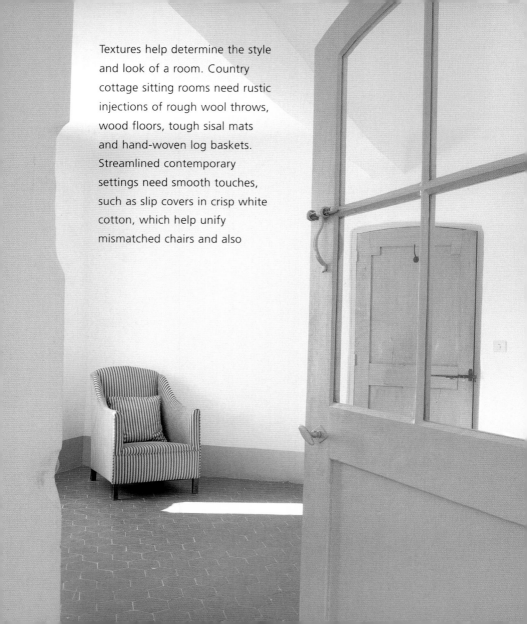

Textures help determine the style and look of a room. Country cottage sitting rooms need rustic injections of rough wool throws, wood floors, tough sisal mats and hand-woven log baskets. Streamlined contemporary settings need smooth touches, such as slip covers in crisp white cotton, which help unify mismatched chairs and also

below and opposite
Comfortable yet functional living spaces with seating covered in robust ticking or calico.

left A small space set aside for a home study area successfully houses vital office elements, including a basic trestle table, a metal filing cabinet, cardboard box files revamped with paint and a smart metal twenties-style desk light.

complement pale wood floors. Modern materials such as zinc and aluminium for lighting and table surfaces also emphasize a more up-to-date look.

Curtains require substantial amounts of fabric but needn't break the bank. Stick to simple headings such as loops and ties. Choose strong cottons and linens. If you buy ten metres or more from many fabric wholesalers they will

relaxed living

99

Simple shapes in plain fabrics create light and airy window treatments:

below Light cotton curtains draped to the floor. They are simply tied onto a metal pole, bought by the length and bent over at the ends.

left Heavy canvas with eyelets can be hooked onto a window frame and pulled back as required.

right Fresh and filmy: soft cream-coloured linen curtains with a decorative double-layered heading, recycled by the owner from a previous apartment. The wooden pole and rings are painted to create a unifying effect.

give you a substantial discount. Line curtains for a better hang and also to give protection from sunlight to prevent fading. Interlinings give greater insulation; bump is the thickest and looks like a blanket, while domette is a brushed cotton and the most commonly used. Roman or roller blinds are useful for providing extra insulation with curtains, as well as protecting from the sun. Blinds also suit just about any window shape. I like Roman blinds and have examples in checked cotton and plain calico hanging at my Georgian sash windows; these are all hand washable in the bath. Unlined curtains in filmy textures such as muslin and organdie are cheap, stylish options.

If you live in a climate with hot summers and cold winters, have sets of light curtains for summer and warmer pairs of thermal ones for winter, as you do for underwear. Paint curtain poles the same colour as walls for a unifying effect. Very cheap ideas for poles include wooden dowelling from timber yards cut to length and painted, and stretchy wire which is ideal for small drops, for example in cottage windows, and available from hardware and DIY shops.

sleeping in style

We do so much of it that sleep deserves to be a peaceful and luxuriating experience. On a cold winter's night it is bliss to curl up in crisp white bedlinen and warm woolly blankets. Conversely, in summer it's good to lie with the sparest of bedclothes, say just a fine cotton sheet, and an open window to catch a cooling night-time breeze. Bedrooms need to be quiet airy refuges away from domestic distractions. There should be lots of cupboards, boxes or ample wardrobe space to stow away clothing and clutter. Some of the best ideas include capacious built-in walk-in wardrobes with simple panelled doors. Old laundry baskets, big wooden boxes and even old shoe boxes covered in fabric and paint are also useful bedroom storage notions. Bedroom textures need to be soft and inviting, such as filmy muslin curtains, plain calico blinds and fine cotton pyjamas. Soft wool blankets in creams or blues are great for dressing beds. Then there are antique quilts with pretty floral sprigged designs, that look lovely folded or draped over a bedstead. Spend as much as you can afford on bedding – soft goosedown duvets and pillows are the ultimate bedtime luxury. It is also prudent to invest in a well-sprung mattress.

Comfort factors in bedrooms include freshly laundered sheets and warm creamy coloured wool blankets. Trawl markets and second-hand shops for old bedlinen; the quality is often better than modern textures. Really worth looking out for are old damask bed covers and fine embroidered linen pillowcases. Sleep peacefully in a traditional bedstead: classic brass always looks wonderful, and decorative ironwork looks great painted white. Create an oasis of calm with a clutter-free room.

A bedroom is a sanctuary, away from work and other people; it is a place where you can tuck yourself up in between crisp sheets with a good book to read, a drink, and a bar of chocolate. Asleep or not, all of us spend so much time there that it should be the one room in the house where we can be indulgent. Bedroom textures should be luxurious, soft and warm. The stresses of the day fall away when you clamber into white cotton sheets, curl up under soft blankets and hug a comforting hot water bottle in cold weather. It pays to invest in the best bedding you can afford and take time in choosing the right bed.

There are all sorts of bed shapes to suit the look you want to achieve. At a basic level there is a divan which can be dressed quite simply, useful in bedrooms that double up as daytime sitting rooms or studies.

I prefer bright and airy bedrooms in whites and creams, in other words rooms that have a light ambience throughout the year. Bedrooms need to be comfortable, optimistic places, with soft bedside lighting, some sort of seating, and maybe a jug of scented flowers.

There is nothing to beat the simplicity of plain white bedlinen. It is smart and unassuming. When an injection of colour is desired then you can look to bold, contemporary designs, perhaps in tomato red, lime green, fuchsia pink or lemon yellow. These sorts of bedlinens work particularly well in southern climates with strong light. It seems that English country-house style with its fussy floral patterned sheets and pillowcases have had their day on the decoration scene (and not too soon). But at the mass-market end of things manufacturers persist in launching frilly, flowery designs that make beds look like the covers of chocolate boxes. However, florals in the bedroom can look really pretty, if used carefully and with restraint. Take as an example a simple lavender-coloured

country bedroom theme, suitable say for a cottage bedroom. You can make up basic pillowcases in a delicate rose-bud print (note that dress fabrics often have more subtle floral designs than their furnishing counterparts) and combine with white sheets and pillowcases and a faded antique floral patchwork quilt. Stick to a plain cotton window treatment, paint the walls white and cover the floors in cheap, neutral cotton rugs. The whole effect is stylish and not in the least bit overdone.

left Grey paintwork and a simple painted bedside table, together with a subtlely checked blue woollen blanket and a glass of vibrant yellow spring daffodils, add colourful injections to the overall neutral effect created by the white walls and bedlinen in this restful Provençal farmhouse bedroom.

this page Brilliant blues lend a seaside air to a Long Island bedroom. Blue-and-white patchwork quilts, boldly striped cotton pillowcases, and white painted walls add to the bright and breezy feel.

right A romantic mahogany *bateau lit* is a great vehicle for layer upon layer of wonderful white antique bedlinen. A filmy mosquito net, functional as well as decorative, is generously swathed from the ceiling to complete the translucent effect.

this page Distinctive in texture and colour, smooth polished parquet flooring and bentwood furniture are smart, dark contrasts to creamy walls and bedlinen in a Paris flat.

Forced to make my bed from an early age, I think that an orderly, uncluttered bedroom helps to set you up mentally for whatever difficulties and chaos you may come across during the day. Storage, of course, is a key issue. It is quite surprising how a few pieces of casually flung clothing, or perhaps a modest pile of discarded newspapers, is all it takes to create a bedroom scene that begins to look like a jumble sale.

A built-in run of shelves with doors along one wall is a very successful way of stowing away clothes, hats, shoes, bags, suitcases and other unavoidable clutter. Free-standing armoires and wardrobes are useful, but impractical if space is tight. If you are restricted to a limited budget then you can curtain off an alcove with calico, linen or even an old bedspread. Save for a couple of hours spent at the sewing machine,

the results are almost instantaneous and very stylish. A large chest of drawers is always useful for swallowing up smaller items of clothing and spare bedlinen. Old trunks, big boxy laundry baskets and modern-looking zinc boxes are also useful bedroom storage devices.

Bedsteads offer a variety of decorative possibilities. A Shaker-style painted wooden four-poster frame looks good with tie-on curtains, a muslin or linen pelmet, or left entirely bare. Good value examples are available in flat-pack kit form.

left A country feel is evoked by matt-painted panelling, wood boards, a painted wooden bed, and simple fabrics and furnishings in a Georgian townhouse. An antique lavender patchwork quilt with a seaweed design and pink sprigged floral pillowcases, run up in lawn dress fabric, provide fresh detail.

Nineteenth-century French metal daybeds are excellent for bed-sitting rooms and look really smart with ticking bolsters and pillows; they are not difficult to find if you track down dealers who specialize in antique French decorative furniture. If you have children in the family then consider pine bunk beds. Available from most department stores or large furniture warehouses, they are very good value and can be dressed up with a coat of paint.

Those of us who enjoy the pleasures of a firm bed know high-quality bedding really does help towards getting a good night's sleep. The best type of mattress is sewn to size

sleeping in style

this page Hot shots: vivid splashes of bright colour work well in sunny, southern climates. Experiment with cool cotton bedlinen in bold blues, greens, yellows, pinks and orange. As temperatures soar, practical ideas for keeping cool are essential: windows flung wide let air flow through, light muslin curtains help to catch a breeze and stone floor tiles stay cool underfoot.

far right Bunk beds are an economical and useful idea for children's bedrooms and are popular for their space-saving qualities as well as being fun to sleep in. Update and give a stylish look to plain pine bunks with pale eggshell paint as seen here.

with layers of white curled feather, together with fleece wool and white cotton felt all incorporated with solid box springs. Perfect pillows are combinations of duck down and feather, grey duck feather, or the ultimate luxury, white goose feather. And for people with allergies there are special hog and cattle hair versions available. It is well worth your while spending that little bit more when it comes to buying bedding, both for increased comfort and longevity.

My dream is to sleep in daily pressed and laundered linen sheets. Until this fantasy is realized I remain content with a box of assorted cotton linens at various stages of wear and tear. My softest sheets are in Egyptian cotton, bought years ago, and still going strong. I also love antique bedlinen and have various Victorian linen and cotton lace pillow-cases, as well as the odd linen sheet handed down from elderly relatives. Although pure linen sheets are costly, and need extra care and maintenance,

they will last a lifetime. When buying linen it should feel clean, starched, crisp and tightly woven.

Duvets have become an almost universal item of bedding, but sheets and blankets have been making a bit of a comeback recently. The practical thing about layers of bed clothes is that you can simply peel back or pull on the layers to suit the temperature. In summer, for example, a cotton blanket and sheet are all that is necessary and if the temperature suddenly plummets then there is nothing to beat the addition of a traditional wool blanket.

clean living

To start the day, an invigorating shower, or simply a wash in a basin of hot water, wakes you up and triggers circulation. At other times, and especially at the end of the day, I can spend hours soaking in a tub of steaming hot water listening to the radio (sneaking off for a mid-afternoon session is also highly recommended for a rare treat). They may not be the best at conserving heat but smooth cast-iron baths are definitely the most agreeable to soak in. It's good to scent the water with fragrant oil or work up a creamy lather with soap. A bleached wooden bath rack is a useful vehicle for storing soaps and flannels and keeping reading material dry and readily to hand. Loofahs, sponges and brushes are also essential bathroom tools for keeping skin pristine and well scrubbed. To accompany daily washing rituals, use fluffy towels in white, seaside blues and bright spring green colours. Soft towelling bathrobes are also a delicious way of drying off – buy big sizes for wrapping up well. The best showers soak you with a powerful delivery, and have finely tuned taps that deliver hot or cold water as you require it. Keep bathrooms well ventilated to clear steam, and invest in duckboards and bathmats to mop up pools of water.

A bath, a shower, or even a quick face splash are instant revivers and help relieve the stresses of daily living. Like eating, washing can be a deliciously sensual ritual. It can vary from a short, sharp, invigorating cold outdoor shower on a hot summer's day to a more languid experience in mid-winter when a long, hot, steaming bath is the perfect antidote to dark days and icy temperatures. Copious supplies of hot water are at the top of my list of crucial bathroom ingredients even the meanest, most poky, drab little bathroom can be acceptable if it delivers piping-hot water, and plenty of it. Smelly soaps and lotions are essential elements too. Among my favourites are delicately scented rosewater soap and rose geranium bath gel. If I'm in the mood for more pungent aromas, I choose stronger-scented spicy soaps with warming tones.

White bathrooms are bright, light and airy, as shown by the gleaming examples seen here. Walls and woodwork are in varying shades of white together with pristine clean ceramic tiles, baths and sinks. Deliciously tactile textures include big fluffy towels, soft sponges and tough cottons for laundry bags.

right Real forties bathrooms were cold clammy places with peeling linoleum floors and intermittent hot water issued from unpredictable gas boilers. The sea green and white Long Island bathroom here might be retro in feeling, but is very modern in its comforting supplies of heat and hot water. Simple and functional, it houses a sturdy cast-iron bath on ball-and-claw feet, a plain wooden mirrored bath cabinet and a painted stool for resting a bathtime drink. Seek out ideas for recreating this relaxed, utilitarian look by rummaging around in second-hand shops for big white clinical enamel jugs (the sort that hospitals used for washing babies), old formica-topped tables, metal buckets and medicine cabinets, or old versions of the wooden bathmat above.

More luxurious yet eminently achievable bathroom ideas include a tinkly glass candelabra for bathing by candlelight, and a comfy chair with soft towelling seating. Practical bathroom storage ideas include woven cane laundry baskets and junk objects like old metal school shoe lockers or tin boxes used to house soaps, lotions and other paraphernalia.

Indispensible for drying off big white cotton bath sheets and white rag-rug Portuguese bath mats is my thirties-style heated chrome towel rail. To finish off the ablutions it's good to wrap up in a soft, white waffle cotton dressing gown – they're rather expensive, but well worth it for a daily dose of luxury.

Choosing a bath is a question of taste as well as practical considerations. Traditional-style, free-standing cast-iron baths with ball and claw feet are deep and look good but they do need sturdy floors to support their own weight, the considerable weight of a bathful of water, plus the weight of the bather. In contrast, modern acrylic baths are light, warm to the touch and come in lots of shapes.

Enamelled steel baths are strong and hardwearing but, like modern acrylic baths, they need the support of a frame. For stylish details either box in the bath with plain white tiles, or make a surround of tongue-and-groove wood panels which can be painted or waxed for protection.

Bathroom textures and surfaces need to be hardwearing and easy to maintain. Cleaning the bathroom becomes less of a chore if you wipe down baths and washbasins daily.

Old ceramic jugs, weathered wooden shelves with cut-out patterns, cheap painted peg rails and seashell prints are key elements for a traditional feel.

Get the look and create your own Georgian-inspired bathroom with sludgy matt eggshell paint, an old-fashioned bath on a raised platform and big weathered brass taps. Hide elements of contemporary life behind plain panelled cupboards. Seal wooden floors in matt varnish or use thick cotton bathmats to soak up water from dripping bodies.

above Daily ablutions are an uplifting experience in this bright and cheery sea green and blue theme. Solid functional fittings that were happily left intact for the owner included a splendid old ceramic sink on a stand with classic taps and visible fittings.

Ceramic sinks, basins, lavatories and shower trays are widely available, and good value. Ceramic tiles for floors and walls provide a good splash-proof environment. Wooden floors are acceptable if well sealed, as is terracotta, or even linoleum, provided it is properly laid to stop water seeping underneath and causing damp. Avoid carpet as sooner or later it will get wet, and begin to turn mouldy and smelly.

The average bathroom showroom stocks a pretty paltry selection of taps and unremarkable shapes often cost the earth. Here are some inspiring ideas.

far left A single stainless steel spout with an artfully concealed tap mechanism.

above Brass taps from a builder's yard.

left Chunky Victorian pillar taps found in a London salvage yard.

clean living

123

opposite Introduce colour to bathrooms with bright towels and marine-blue and lime-green robes.

right Swimming-pool inspired tiny blue mosaic tiles are an inventive idea for a walk-in shower space. Equally resourceful are basic stainless steel kitchen mixer taps reinvented as shower taps and spouts.

When planning a shower it is essential to check that you have enough water pressure to produce a powerful downpour. You might need a pump that automatically boosts the flow. Showers can be simple affairs – from a hand set fitted to the bath taps with a protective screen or curtain, to a state-of-the-art walk-in room with a shower that delivers deluges of water.

There are numerous ways of storing bathroom equipment. Built-in cupboards are useful and one which houses a boiler will make practical airing-cupboard space for keeping hot, dry towels to hand. Boxes and baskets are good for stowing away dirty linen, spare towels or bathroom brushes and sponges. Versatile peg racks in wood and metal are ideal for hanging up sponge bags and flannels.

outdoor living

When the temperature rises and the days lengthen images of summer reappear: like sand between the toes, warm bare skin, icy drinks and creased cool linen, and it's time to head outside. Dedicated lovers of the outdoors will already have grabbed the pleasures of those first few tentative days of spring when it's a revelation to feel and see the sun again after months of dreary winter. They pack up picnic baskets and rugs and head off for the first coast or countryside excursion of the season. Given a sunny day and appropriate clothing I will pack up a thermos of hot soup, smoked salmon and cream cheese bagels and head off with my family to an empty stretch of south coast beach.

Then, when summer is well established there is that feeling that it will go on forever and everyone becomes complacent and even irritated with the heat and humidity. But what luxury when the days are long and the evenings balmy to eat breakfast, lunch, tea or supper al fresco. Invigorating as well as relaxing, the event can be as simple as a coffee taken at a pavement café – something blissful for gardenless city dwellers – or a weekend picnic in the park with friends, sharing the best cheese, bread and wine affordable.

outdoor living

Eating outside is one of life's sensual pleasures. Whatever the scenario, from a windswept beach beneath racing clouds to a warm jasmine-scented Mediterranean night, food seems to develop in taste and texture when eaten out in the elements.

The British, for instance, have always been keen on picnics, packing up thermos flasks, rugs, raincoats and quantities of ham sandwiches to face unpredictable weather with determination. In complete contrast, the southern Spaniards give in to

left Keep cool with a shady awning made from sheets of cane spread over a simple iron framework. Other ideas for retreating out of the sun include panels of striped or plain canvas stretched hammock-style across a small courtyard, patio or between trees. For a more permanent arrangement that can be stored over the winter months, invest in a big canvas umbrella on metal or wooden frames. I've seen good ones in basic green-and-white stripes, designed for use on the beach but equally at home in the back garden or country.

right The only rule for food served outside is that is should be delicious and easy to eat.

fiercely hot summer afternoons and laze around shady tables idling over jamón, bread, wine and steaming paellas cooked up on portable primus stoves.

The passion for eating *al fresco* has grown with me into adult life. Childhood picnics are remembered for their delicious informality, where for once adults didn't bother with cutlery or insist on elbows being off the table, or even mind if you sprawled sandwich in hand. In summer, inspired by books such as Elizabeth David's *Summer Cooking*, my picnics might include baguettes soaked with olive oil and garlic, stuffed with goats' cheese and anchovies. All this is stored in one of those not very sightly, but eminently practical, plastic cool boxes, together with drinks of beer, bubbly Cava or crisp dry Manzanilla sherry.

At home my tiny backyard becomes an extra room in summer. There is not much sun, but climbing roses and clematis manage to thrive, and flower pots filled with herbs add colour, texture and culinary detail. As soon as the temperature allows, we set up a big wooden table and green metal folding chairs. I like to spread the table with white or blue-and-white check cloths together with jars of nasturtiums or cow parsley. In the evening, candles set in pots provide a wonderful glow and they don't blow out.

outdoor living

When I am able to visit a good fishmonger we eat barbecued salmon steaks, sardines, or mackerel stuffed with parsley, lemon and garlic. For pudding I sometimes make strawberry or raspberry ice cream with the help of a small electric ice cream machine, and serve it with summer berries and hunks of shortbread.

Equipment for eating out in the open has never been so varied. Chain stores stock bright plastic picnic kits that are great value. Sleek, streamlined and shatter-proof stainless flasks that keep fluids hot or cold are also useful. Furniture ideas include fold-up slatted chairs that can be stowed away easily in winter. If your funds don't run to an expensive garden table then cheat with an old door laid across trestles, and cover it with a cloth in a favourite fabric.

Durable, portable and attractive outdoor ideas: folding wooden tables and chairs (these were borrowed from the local village bar in Spain but similar ones can be found in second-hand furniture shops); lengths of cotton for tablecloths, cushions for comfort; bright yellow plastic tumblers; woven olive baskets; and jars packed with freshly picked herbs for decoration.

credits

page 1 checked cotton Ikea; jug Heal's; tea towels Crate & Barrel, USA

page 2 room painted in Nantucket Benjamin Moore USA

page 4 Provençal chairs Paris junk shop

page 6 cotton drill Z. Butt Textiles

page 7 interior design Susie Manby

page 10 enamel jugs Ruby Beets Antiques, USA

page 11 ribbed glass The Conran Shop; candles Price's Candles

page 14 tea towels Wolfman Gold & Good Co., USA; chair cover fabric Laura Ashley; plates and jugs from a selection at Pottery Barn, USA; bowl Habitat

page 15 paint swatches from top: Sanderson Spectrum 22-1 Lavender White, Sanderson Spectrum 7-13 Marble White; Sanderson Spectrum 4-10 Winter White, Dulux 0005-Y Tremble, Dulux 0705-Y Sunbleached, Sanderson Spectrum 04-09 Neutral

page 16 paint swatches from top: John Oliver Winter Sky, Dulux 1520-B10G Relaxation, Sanderson Spectrum 26-04 Lupine Blue, Dulux 1030-R80B Bridesmaid, Sanderson Spectrum 24-11 Wood Hyacinth; plastic beaker Heal's

page 17 striped table mat Crate & Barrel; junk chair painted in Sanderson Spectrum 24-04 Swiss blue eggshell; plate Anta; checked tray John Lewis

page 18 paint swatches from top: Sanderson Spectrum 41-03

Springtime, Sanderson Spectrum 40-04 Sunny Green, Sanderson Spectrum 39-03 Salad Green, Dulux 1520-G Lily Root, Farrow & Ball 23 Powder Blue, Farrow & Ball 32 Cooking Apple Green

page 19 coffee cup and saucer Designers Guild

page 20 paint swatches from bottom: Sanderson Spectrum 23-09 Fascination, Sanderson Spectrum 21-10 Fidelity, Sanderson Spectrum 21-17 Lavender Lave, Sanderson Spectrum 21-04 Lilac, Dulux 1040-R70B Harlequin; lavender paper and folder from a selection at Paperchase; plastic brush Designers Guild

page 21 Bunny chair Designers Guild; cushion fabric Manuel Canovas

page 22 napkins Habitat

page 23 paint swatches from bottom: Dulux 2030-Y70R Campfire, Farrow & Ball 39 Fowler Pink, Farrow & Ball 45 Sand, Dulux 3050-Y50R Free Range, Sanderson Spectrum 50-23 Salisbury; pots Clifton Nurseries

page 24 chair cover fabric Habitat; wall painted in Country Cream, Dulux

page 25 paint swatches from top: Dulux 0030-Y10R Jigsaw, Dulux 1030-Y Spring Butter, Farrow & Ball 44 Cream, Sanderson Spectrum 6-23 Gobi Tan, Farrow & Ball 15 Bone; throw Colefax & Fowler

pages 26–27 plate Ruby Beets Antiques, USA

page 28 galvanized metal storage box Ikea; wooden and metal cutlery from a selection at Wolfman Gold & Good Co., USA

page 30 sisal mat John Lewis

pages 36–37 fabrics from top: cotton stripe; cotton check; cotton check; cotton check (all by Designers Guild); plain green cotton The Conran Shop, cotton roller towel by Universal Towel Company; cotton by The Conran Shop; cotton mix stripe by John Lewis; cotton ticking by Russell & Chapple; cotton check by Ikea; cotton ticking by Ian Mankin; cotton stripe by Laura Ashley

pages 38–39 1 cotton sheeting John Lewis 2 cotton voile Wolfin Textiles 3 cotton Muriel Short 4 polyester/cotton muslin Laura Ashley 5 cotton muslin Wolfin Textiles 6 cotton stripe The Conran Shop 7 cotton check The Conran Shop 8 cotton check The Conran Shop 9 self-checked cotton voile Habitat 10 silk Pongees 11 cotton voile check Habitat 12 cotton voile Laura Ashley 13 printed cotton tana lawn Liberty 14 cotton chambray McCulloch & Wallis 15 cotton calico Wolfin Textiles 16 cotton Wolfin Textiles 17 cotton muslin Muriel Short 18 cotton stripe Ian Mankin 19 cotton Habitat 20 cotton Designers Guild 21 polyester/cotton muslin Laura Ashley 22 linen Wolfin Textiles 23 natural linen Wolfin Textiles 24 cotton muslin Muriel Short 25 cotton muslin Muriel Short 26 cotton The Conran Shop 27 cotton voile check Designers Guild 28 voile check Designers Guild 29 cotton striped voile Habitat

pages 40–41 30 printed cotton Cath Kidston 31 wool mix felt J.W.Bollom

132

32 cotton stripe The Blue Door 33 cotton stripe Pukka Palace 34 cotton check Colefax & Fowler 35 cotton check Colefax & Fowler 36 cotton stripe The Blue Door 37 cotton stripe Habitat 38 cotton chambray R. Halstuk 39 linen check The Blue Door 40 cotton ticking Ian Mankin 41 cotton stripe The Blue Door 42 printed floral cotton Manuel Canovas 43 cotton viscose check Manuel Canovas 44 cotton check The Blue Door 45 cotton stripe The Malabar Cotton Co. 46 cotton stripe Habitat 47 printed cotton stripe Laura Ashley 48 & 49 linen herringbone The Blue Door 50 pink cotton check Ian Mankin 51 green cotton check Ian Mankin 52 & 53 cotton checks Ian Mankin 54 printed cotton floral Jane Churchill 55 linen The Blue Door 56 cotton check Habitat 57 cotton check Designers Guild 58 cotton check Ikea 59 cotton check Habitat 60 cotton check Ian Mankin 61 cotton check Designers Guild 62 cotton check Ian Mankin 63 & 64 cotton checks The Malabar Cotton Co. 65 cotton drill Wolfin Textiles 66 cotton stripe Habitat 67 roller towel Universal Towel Company

pages 42–43 68 cotton mix stripe John Lewis 69 cotton denim Z.Butt Textiles 70 cotton ticking Russell & Chapple 71 & 72 cotton Habitat 73 cotton stripe Designers Guild 74 linen Muriel Short 75 cotton calico Wolfin Textiles 76 cotton Pierre Frey 77 cotton check Ian Mankin 78 check Ian Mankin 79 wool tartan Anta 80 wool check Anta 81 cotton Osborne & Little 82 cotton duck Russell & Chapple 83 cotton canvas Wolfin Textiles 84 cotton gingham daisy Sanderson 85 cotton check Designers Guild 86 cotton check

Habitat 87 self-patterned cotton/viscose Marvic Textiles 88, 89 & 90 cotton Osborne & Little 91 cotton The Conran Shop 92 cotton check Designers Guild 93 cotton gingham daisy Sanderson 94 cotton check Habitat 95 cotton check Colefax & Fowler 96 linen Wolfin Textiles

pages 44–45 chairs left to right painted in 39-03 salad green eggshell Sanderson Spectrum; covered in floral cotton print Manuel Canovas; painted in 24-04 Swiss blue eggshell Sanderson Spectrum; painted in 21-10 fidelity Sanderson Spectrum

page 46 counter clockwise from top: Bunny chair Designers Guild; pine Lantula dining room table Ikea; junk shop chair, fabric Cath Kidston; folding chair The Reject Shop; factory chair After Noah

page 47 clockwise from top: zinc-top table Cath Kidston; Montecarlo chair The Conran Shop; metal table The Conran Shop; white folding chair Ikea; wooden kitchen table Decorative Living; stool Habitat; peasant beech chair McCord; folding chair The Reject Shop; church chair Castle Gibson; birchwood ply trestle table McCord; centre: table Ikea painted in Colour World E5-16 Bromel eggshell, J. W. Bollom

page 48 above: Douglas Fir bed in Pawson House, London, designed by John Pawson; left: four-poster bed frame Ikea; right: wrought iron bed After Noah

page 49 clockwise from top: Coward sofa SCP; Swedish cot sofa Sasha Waddell; armchair George Smith

page 50 kitchen units Ikea

page 51 metal mesh wardrobe Action Handling Equipment; cotton accessory bags Hold Everything, USA; wardrobe junk shop; dresser Colette Aboudaram, France

pages 52–53 Misu glass tumblers Ikea; metal mesh basket Crate & Barrel, USA

page 54 clockwise from top: stainless steel pedal bin Divertimenti; garlic crusher, whisk, crab crackers Divertimenti; glass lemon squeezer Woolworths; kettle Staines Catering

page 55 clockwise from top: Le Pentole steamer Divertimenti; Le Creuset pot, Divertimenti; fish kettle Gill Wing; colander Woolworths; espresso maker McCord; cutlery McCord; corkscrew Divertimenti; scissors John Lewis; Sabatier stainless steel knife Divertimenti; grater Divertimenti; sieve Divertimenti; Le Pentole frying pan Divertimenti

page 56 clockwise from top: candle holder Habitat; pendant light After Noah; nightlights Ikea; lantern Habitat

page 57 anglepoise lamp After Noah

page 58 galvanized steel storage boxes Muji; shoe rack Ikea; clothes rail B.S. Sales

page 59 clockwise from top: buckets The Conran Shop and hardware stores; butchers hooks Divertimenti; glass storage jars Divertimenti; laundry basket Tobias and the Angel; blue and green cotton fabric The Conran Shop; blanket Melin Tregwynt; beaker

Muji; shoe boxes fabric Manuel Canovas; J. W. Bollom; peg rail Ikea

page 60 shadow boxes Habitat

page 61 pudding basins Divertimenti; picture frames Habitat

page 62 clockwise from top: cream cup and saucer by Veronique Pichon at Designers Guild; Poole pottery jug Designers Guild; Champagne flute The Conran Shop; Duralex tumbler Spanish supermarket; ripple glass Designers Guild; tumbler Crate & Barrel, USA; tumbler Pottery Barn, USA; Misu tumbler Ikea; mug Habitat; white coffee cup and saucer Habitat; blue-and-white china Crate & Barrel, USA

page 63 clockwise from top: tartan plate Anta; Cornishware plate Heal's gingham bowl McCord; blue-and-white bowl Habitat; spotty bowl Designers Guild; jug Divertimenti; white plate Wedgwood

pages 66–67 enamel jug Ruby Beets Antiques, USA

pages 68–69 saucepans Brick Lane Market; tartan plates Anta; sink and taps Aston Matthews

pages 70–71 Swedish stove Jotul; interior design Susie Manby

pages 72–73 Kilner jars After Noah; cake tins Brick Lane Market; white metal chair Brimfield Market USA

pages 74–75 chair cover fabric similar at Universal Towel Company; white bowls from a selection at Wolfman Gold & Good Co., USA

page 76 Provençal chairs Paris junk shop

page 77 above: table and chairs similar at After Noah; flower pots Clifton Nurseries; white china Gill Wing

page 78 white plates Wedgwood

page 79 chair cover fabric Russell & Chapple; metal table The Conran Shop; curtain fabric Designers Guild; lilac paint Sanderson spectrum vinyl matt emulsion Fascination 2309M

pages 80–81 left: wicker parlour chairs Palecek; myrtle topiary Christian Tortu at Takashimaya; white table junk shop; right: laminated Saarinen table and Tulip chair Frank Lord

pages 82–83 above left: loft dining area by James Lynch; below left and right: room and furniture in Pawson House, London, designed by John Pawson

pages 84–85 blind fabric Colefax & Fowler; plastic tablecloth John Lewis; wool throw Anta; chandelier Robert Davies; wall paint Country Cream Dulux

pages 86–87 sofa fabric Sanderson; green cotton check cushion Laura Ashley; cushion in blue cotton The Conran Shop; cushions in blue check JAB; throw Anta

pages 88–89 fabric swatches: narrow and wide cotton stripes Habitat; cotton check The Conran Shop; main picture: floral cotton covers, striped cotton blinds, linen and cotton rug Ralph Lauren, USA; ticking cushion fabric Ralph Lauren, USA and antique samples; right: metal daybed Colette Aboudaram, France; antique ticking on cushion fabric Bryony Thomasson

page 90 blue cotton sofa fabric The Conran Shop, Paris; terracotta cotton armchair fabric Ian Mankin; interior design by Susie Manby

page 91 above: paint Olive and Calke Green matt emulsion mixed together Farrow & Ball, candle holder and side cupboard After Noah; main picture: chair and sofa cover, cotton rug and paint Ralph Lauren, USA; cushion cover fabric Designers Guild

pages 92–93 main picture: blinds in checked cotton Designers Guild; wing chair covered in Tulipan Marvic textiles; cream paint Buttermilk Dulux; white table Brick Lane market; right: checked terracotta fabric on sofa Manuel Canovas; wooden chest and metal planter Tobias and The Angel; Butler's tray table Crate & Barrel, USA, painted in Sanderson Spectrum Satinwood 50-23

page 94 light Lieux, Paris; wool appliqué cover Siécle, Paris;

page 95 left: basket chair Alfies Antique Market; mirror from Cligoncourt Market, Paris; right: wall paint colour Nantucket, Benjamin Moore USA

pages 96–97 main picture: wool blankets Anta; cotton rugs Habitat; cupboard Ikea; checked cotton chair covers Ian Mankin; chairs A Barn Full of Sofas and Chairs; chandelier Wilchester County; shades The Dining Room Shop

page 98 chair in antique ticking Bryony Thomasson; interior design Susie Manby

page 99 filing cabinet B.S. Sales; trestle table McCord; filing boxes, frames Ikea; metal chair and cover in cotton check Habitat; Bunny chair Designers Guild; wastepaper basket The Conran Shop; sofa Ikea

page 100 below: curtain fabric The Conran Shop

page 101 linen curtain fabric from a selection Rosebrand Textiles, USA; myrtle tree Christian Tortu at Takashimaya,

New York; sofa from a barn sale; wall paint Nantucket Benjamin Moore, USA

page 104 bed Portobello Road Market; chair Alfies Antique Market; white paint John Oliver

page 105 old linen Judy Greenwood

page 106 table Colette Aboudaram, France

page 107 striped cotton pillowcase Ralph Lauren, USA; patchwork quilt on bed Ruby Beets Antiques, USA; quilt on wall, Brimfield Market, USA

page 108 Tom Dixon light Gladys Mougin, Paris; Indian cotton bedspread Living Tradition, Paris

page 109 mosquito net Mombasa Net Canopies, USA

page 110 bed Jim Howitt; antique quilt Judy Greenwood; pillowcases in cotton lawn Liberty; linen fabric on seat cushions Laura Ashley; white bedlinen John Lewis; paint Dulux Sandstone eggshell

page 111 bolster pad John Lewis; cotton striped fabric Laura Ashley; wooden box Tobias and The Angel

page 112 muslin curtains Pottery Barn, USA; bedlinen Designers Guild; wool blanket Melin Tregwynt

page 113 bunkbeds Habitat Paris

page 116 above: shower curtain similar at Crate & Barrel, USA; below left: drawstring bag fabric Russell & Chapple; starfish Eaton Shell Shop

page 117 antique cupboard Colette Aboudaram, France; interior design Susie Manby

page 118 wooden duckboard Habitat

page 119 above left: peg rail Robert Davies; chair Alfies

Antique Market; above right: linen basket Habitat top; below: shoe rack, pine mirror, butcher's hooks After Noah; brushes, soaps The Conran Shop; towels Muji; galvanized bucket The Conran Shop; medicine bottles junk shop

page 120 jug from a selection at Sage St Antiques, USA; peg rail Ikea

page 121 taps and bath Lassco; wooden bath rack Habitat; towels John Lewis

page 122 nail brush John Lewis; below: tap and stone basin in Pawson House, London, designed by John Pawson

page 123 main picture: taps and bath Lassco; bath rack Habitat; right: outdoor brass taps from builders' merchants

page 124 bathroom by James Lynch; bath Lassco; shower taps Nicholls and Clarke; tins Alfies Antique Market

page 125 left: towels, flannels and robe Designers Guild; right: towels John Lewis

pages 126–127 cutlery Designers Guild; beaker Heal's; blanket Anta; table Brick Lane Market

page 129 tablecloth fabric Designers Guild; chair and table Clifton Nurseries

page 130–131 beakers Heal's; tablecloth fabric and cushions Designers Guild

Please note that credits were correct at time of photography but availability of items shown may have changed.

suppliers

bedlinen

Cologne & Cotton,
791 Fulham Rd, London
SW6 5HD (mail order)
www.cologneandcotton.com
Beautiful bedlinen in plain white and colours; also towels and robes.

Damask, Broxholme House,
New King's Rd, London SW6 4AA
www.damask.co.uk
Cotton bedlinen plus accessories.

Designers Guild, 267 King's Rd,
London SW3 5EN
www.designersguild.com
The best brightly coloured cotton bedlinen designs around.

Judy Greenwood Antiques,
657 Fulham Rd, London SW6 5PY
Antique patchwork quilts, old white damask bed covers and antique beds.

Habitat, 196 Tottenham Court
Rd, London W1T 7LG
www.habitat.co.uk
Really good cotton sheets in variety of colours, plus throws and bedcovers.

Heal's, 196 Tottenham Court
Rd, London W1T 7LQ
www.heals.co.uk
Really good quality beds, white cotton sheets, luxurious duvets and pillows.

Ikea, 2 Drury Way, North
Circular Rd, London NW10 0TH
www.ikea.co.uk
Good range of bedframes, including bunks and a stylish, simple four poster.

The Monogrammed Linen Shop,
168 Walton St, London SW3 2JL
www.monogrammedlinenshop.com
*Pillows and sheets embroidered
with your initials.*

The Shaker Shop, 72
Marylebone High St, W1U 5JW
*Simple checked bedlinen, plus
Shaker style beds.*

Tobias and The Angel, 68 White
Hart Lane, London SW13
*Antique linen: old linen
pillowcases, and sheets, plus
antique wooden bedsteads.*

Melin Tregwynt, Castlemorris,
Haverfordwest, Pembrokeshire
SA62 5UX
www.melintregwynt.co.uk
*Checked wool blankets in blues,
greens and yellows.*

The White Company,
www.thewhitecompany.co.uk
White bedlinen, pure linen.

fabric

Anta, Fearn, Tain, Ross, Scotland
IV20 1XW and 55 Sloane Sq,
London SW1W 8AX
www.anta.co.uk
*Boldly coloured tartans in wool
and silk.*

Laura Ashley, 256–258 Regent
St, London W1R 5DA
www. lauraashley. com

*Wide
selection of
coloured
cotton in
prints and
weaves; also
upholstery
linen.*

The Blue Door, 74 Church Rd,
Barnes, London SW13 0DQ
www.thebluedoor.co.uk
*Blue-and-white Swedish checks,
stripes and plains in cotton and
linen.*

Jane Churchill, 151 Sloane St,
London SW1X 9BX
Decorative cottons.

Colefax and Fowler, 39 Brook
St, London W1K 4JE
*Traditional floral and checked
cotton.*

The Conran Shop, Michelin
House, 81 Fulham Rd, London
SW3 6RD
www.conran.co.uk
*Brightly coloured Indian cottons
plus wide range of other cotton
textures.*

Designers Guild, 267 King's Rd,
London SW3 5EN
www.designersguild.com
*The best brightly coloured cotton
bedlinen designs around.*

Habitat, 196 Tottenham Court
Rd, London W1T 7LG
www.habitat.co.uk
*Good cotton sheets in variety of
colours, plus throws and bedcovers.*

JAB International, Chelsea
Harbour Design Centre, London
SW10 0XE
*A wide range of textures and
woven checked cottons.*

Cath Kidston, 8 Clarendon Cross,
London W11 4AP and branches
www.cathkidston.co.uk
Bright floral fiftes-inspired cotton.

Liberty, Regent St, London W1B
5AH
www.liberty.co.uk

*Wide range of furnishing fabrics,
plus floral printed cotton lawn.*

MacCulloch & Wallis, 25–26
Dering St, London W1R 0BH
www.macculloch-wallis.co.uk
*Distributors of Bennett Silks: a
huge variety in creams and bright
colours plus ribbons and bindings.*

Manuel Canovas Sold through
Colefax and Fowler.
*Bold floral prints, and wonderful
coloured weaves for upholstery.*

Malabar Cotton Co., The Coach
House, Bakery Place, 119
Altenburg Gardens, London SW11
www.malabar.co.uk
*Colourful Indian checks, stripes
and plain cottons.*

Marvic Textiles, Unit 1,
Westpoint Trading Estate, Alliance
Rd, Acton, London W3 0RA
www.marvictextiles.co.uk
*Good weaves in wide range of
colours for upholstery.*

Osborne & Little, 304–308
King's Rd, London SW3 5UH
www.osborneandlittle.com
Cottons and upholstery weaves.

Sanderson, 233 King's Rd
London SW3
www.sanderson.co.uk
*Striped and checked cottons for
upholstery and curtains.*

Muriel Short, Hewitts, Elmbridge
Rd, Cranleigh, Surrey GU6 8LW
*Good selection of muslin and
plain linens in bright colours.*

flooring

Crucial Trading, 79 Westbourne
Park Rd, London W2 5QH
www.crucial-trading.com
Floor coverings in coir, sisal and jute.

Fired Earth, 117–19 Fulham Rd, London SW3 6RL and branches. www.firedearth.co.uk
Natural coir and sisal flooring plus all kinds of terracotta flooring.

Hardwood Flooring Co, 146–152 West End Lane, London NW6 1SD www.hardwoodflooringcompany.com
Oak, ash, beech, maple, teak, mahogany, pitchpine.

Ikea, 2 Drury Way, North Circular Rd, London NW10 0TH www.ikea.co.uk
Mats and rugs in wool and cotton, plus laminate and wooden flooring.

Junckers, Unit 3–5, Wheaton Court Commercial Centre, Wheaton Rd, Essex CM8 3UJ www.junckers.com
Tough, stylish wooden strip flooring.

Lassco, 41 Maltby St, London SE1 3PA www.lassco.co.uk
Reclaimed timber, including old oak floorboards, plus stone and terracotta floor tiles.

Roger Oates, The Long Barn, Eastnor, Ledbury, Herefordshire HR8 1EL www.rogeroates.com
Wool runners, mats and rugs.

Paris Ceramics, 583 King's Rd, London SW6 2EH www.parisceramics.com
Stone and terracotta flooring.

Sinclair Till, 791–793 Wandsworth Rd, London SW8 3JQ
Natural floor coverings in coir and sisal, plus wooden and composite floors, and linoleum.

Walcot Reclamation, 108 Walcot St, Bath BA1 5BG www.walcot.com
Hardwood planking, strip, block and parquet flooring, also York stone flags.

food

Carluccio's, 28a Neal St, Covent Garden, London WC2H 9QT www.carluccios.com
Italian breads, pasta, cheese, oils and fresh wild mushrooms.

Steve Hatt, 88–90 Essex Rd, London N1 8LU
The best fresh fish and shellfish.

Neal's Yard Dairy, 17 Shorts Gardens, London WC2H 9UP www.nealsyarddairy.co.uk
Excellent British cheeses.

Monmouth Coffee House, 27 Monmouth St, London WC2 www.monmouthcoffee.co.uk
Really good coffees.

Sierra Rica, www.sierraica.com
Organic foods from Andalucia Spain, chestnuts peeled and cooked, soups and sauces.

London Farmer's Markets, www.lfm.org.uk
Meat, fruit, vegetables, bread and homemade cakes direct from the producers.

furniture/accessories

Action Handling, The Maltings Industrial Estate, Station Rd, Sawbridgeworth, Herts CM21 9JY www.actionhandling.com
Metal mesh storage and office and factory furniture.

Aria, 133 Upper St, London N1 1QP www.ariar-shop.co.uk
Contemporary furniture and accessories.

The Conran Shop, Michelin House, 81 Fulham Rd, London SW3 6RD www.conran.co.uk
Ideas for seating, and dining; great baskets, bath towel, china and lots of outdoor living ideas, such as lanterns, flower pots, folding chairs.

Designers Guild, 267 King's Rd, London SW3 5EN www.designersguild.com
Modern upholstery, painted furniture plus brightly coloured cushions, stationery, tableware and baskets.

Egg, 36, 37 & 69 Kinnerton St, London SW1X 8ES www. eggtrading.com
Simple accessories and fabrics with an ethnic feel.

The Flower Room, Columbia Road, London E2
Room scents, burning oils and pot pourri created by Angela Flanders. Open Sunday mornings.

Habitat, 196 Tottenham Court Rd, London W1T 7LG
www.habitat.co.uk
All sorts of stylish furniture for the home, plus a good selection of frames and shadow boxes, also vases, boxes, baskets and bath towels.

The Holding Co., 243–245 King's Rd, London SW3 5EL
Storage ideas, including hanging canvas holders for shoes and clothes.

Ikea, 2 Drury Way, North Circular Rd, London NW10 0TH
www.ikea.co.uk
Everything for the home at great prices; lots of the furniture is flat-packed for convenience.

McCord Catalogue, Euroway Business Park, Swindon SN5 8SN
Great home basics, including simple trestle tables and kitchen chairs.

Muji, 187 Oxford St, London W1R 1AJ
www.muji.co.uk
Simple furniture and Japanese-style flat-pack cardboard and metal storage boxes, stationery, bedding.

Purves & Purves, 220–224 Tottenham Court Rd, W1T 7QE
www.purves.co.uk
Contemporary furniture and accessories.

Paperchase, 213 Tottenham Court Rd, London W1T 9PS
www.paperchase.co.uk
All kinds of paper sold by the sheet, plus other stationery ideas.

V.V. Rouleaux, 54 Sloane Sq, London SW1 8AW and 6 Marylebone High St, W1M 3PB
www.vvrouleaux.com
Ribbons in all widths, textures and colours.

SCP, 135–139 Curtain Rd, London EC2A 3BX
Contemporary furniture, including modern classic reproductions.

George Smith, 587–589 King's Rd, London SW6 2EH
Well-built, well-sprung upholstery, including really big comfortable sofas.

Viaduct, 1–10 Summer's St, London EC1 5BD
www.viaduct.co.uk
Contemporary furniture.

kitchen/dining

Ideas for equipment, china and glass:

BhS, 252–258 Oxford St, London W1N 9DC
www.bhs.co.uk

The Conran Shop, Michelin House, 81 Fulham Rd, London SW3 6RD
www.conran.co.uk

The Dining Room Shop, 62–64 White Hart Lane, London SW13 0PZ
www.thediningroomshop.co.uk

Divertimenti, 139–141 Fulham Rd, London SW3 6SD
www.divertimenti.co.uk

Graham & Green, 4–7 & 10 Elgin Crescent, London W11 2JA
www.grahamandgreen.co.uk

Habitat, 196 Tottenham Court Rd, London W1T 7LG
www.habitat.co.uk

Ikea, 2 Drury Way, North Circular Rd, London NW10 0TH
www.ikea.co.uk

John Lewis, 278–306 Oxford St, London W1A 1EX
www.johnlewis.com

Liberty, Regent St, London W1B 5AH
www.liberty.co.uk

David Mellor, 4 Sloane Sq, London SW1W 8EE
www.davidmellordesigns.com

The Pier, 200 Tottenham Court Rd, London W1T 7PL
www.pier.co.uk

Peter Jones, Sloane Sq, London SW1W 8EL
www.johnlewis.com

Summerill and Bishop, 100 Portland Rd, London W11 4LN

kitchens and bathroom fittings

CP Hart, Newnham Terrace, Hercules Rd, London, SE1 7DR
www.cphart.co.uk
Taps, sinks, baths of every shape and description.

Lassco, 101–106 Britannia Walk, Islington, London N1
www.lassco.co.uk
Reclaimed baths, old sinks, old chrome taps and shower heads.

Aston Matthews, 141–147 Essex Rd, London, N1 2SN
www.astonmatthews.co.uk
Taps, shower trays, basins, sinks, baths, towel rails.

Nicholls and Clarke, 3–10 Shoreditch High St, London E1 6PE
www.phlexicare.com
Taps, baths, kitchen sinks, etc.

Stovax, Falcon Road, Sowton Industrial Estate, Exeter, EX2 7LF
Distributors of Jotul.

lighting

The Dining Room Shop, 62–64 White Hart Lane, London SW13 0PZ
www.thediningroomshop.co.uk
Checked candle shades and brass candle carriers.

Habitat, 196 Tottenham Court Rd, London W1T 7LG
www.habitat.co.uk
Including desk lights, hanging pendants, lamps and bases.

Ikea, 2 Drury Way, North Circular Rd, London NW10 0TH
www.ikea.co.uk
Range of lighting, from lamps and bases to pendant shapes.

Price's Candles, 100 York Rd, London SW11 3RU
www.prices-candles.co.uk
Huge selection of candles.

Purves & Purves, 220–224 Tottenham Court Rd, W1T 7QE
www.purves.co.uk
Contemporary shapes.

SKK, 19a Islington Park St, London, N1 1QB
www.skk.net
Contemporary lights.

outside

David Austin Roses, Bowling Green Lane, Albrighton, Wolverhampton
www.davidaustinroses.com
Hundreds of varieties.

Chelsea Gardener, 125 Sydney St, London SW3 6NR
Good for plants, pots and furniture.

Clifton Nurseries, 5a Clifton Villas, Little Venice, London W9 2PH
Everything for a well-furnished garden: clematis, honeysuckles, topiary box, herbs, bedding plants; plus huge range of flower pots and trellis.

Columbia Rd Flower Market, London EC2 (Bethnal Green tube)
Held every Sunday morning: a great source of cheap bulbs, cut flowers and plants in season.

Langley Boxwood Nursery, Rake, Nr Liss, Hampshire GU33 7JL
Specialist in decorative box.

The Organic Gardening Catalog, The Riverdene Business Park, Molesey Road, Hersham, Surrey, KT12 4RG
www.organiccatalog.com

Provenance Plants, 1 Guessens Walk, Welwyn Garden City, Herts AL8 6QS
Plants by mail order including foxgloves, lavender and auriculas.

Florists guaranteed to have a good range of seasonal and stylish cut flowers and plants:

Paula Pryke, The Flower House, Cynthia St, London N1 9JF
www.paula-pryke-flowers.com

Wild at Heart, 49a Ledbury Rd, London, W11 2AA

The Flower Van, Michelin House, 81 Fulham Rd, London SW3 6RD

McQueens, 126 St John St, London EC1V 4JS

Jane Packer, 32 New Cavendish St, London, W1G 8UE

paints

Manufacturers with an interesting range of colours:

Farrow & Ball, Uddens Estate, Wimborne, Dorset BH21 7NL
www.farrow-ball.com
National Trust colours, in a range of period shades.

J.W. Bollom, 15 Theobalds Rd, London WC1X 8SN
www.bollom.com

Cole & Son (Wallpapers) Ltd, 144 Offord Rd, Islington London N1
www.cole-and-son.co.uk
Compact range of period paint colours.

Dulux Advice Centre, ICI Paints, Wexham Rd, Slough, SL2 5DS

John Oliver, 33 Pembridge Rd, London W11 3HG
Small range of excellent colours, including bright Chinese yellow.

Sanderson, 112–120 Brompton Rd, London, SW3
www.sanderson-online.co.uk

second hand and markets

After Noah, 121 Upper St, London, N1 1QP
www. afternoah.com
Factory and school-house furniture and accessories, plus own-range spun aluminum pendant lights.

Alfies Antique Market, 13–25 Church St, London NW8 8DT
Everything from sixties furniture to old fabrics, including second-hand chairs, tables, china and glass.

D.A. Binder, 101 Holloway Rd, London N7
Factory and old office furniture.

Castle Gibson, 106a Upper St, London N1 1QN
Factory tables, cupboards, and old office and institutional furniture.

Decorative Living, 55 New King's Rd, London SW6 4SE
www.decorativeliving.co.uk
Array of decorative antique furniture and accessories.

Tobias and The Angel, 68 White Hart Lane, London SW13 0PZ
Decorative country furniture and accessories, including metal watering cans and other gardening equipment.

Markets that yield interesting finds:

Bermondsey, London SE1
(London Bridge tube)
Held early Friday morning: antiques plus junk furniture and accessories.

Brick Lane, London E1 (Liverpool St tube) *Held every Sunday morning: junk chairs, tables, kitchenware.*

Portobello Road, London W11 (Notting Hill Tube)
Held every Friday & Saturday: sprawling array of stalls selling junk furniture and accessories.

foreign sources

Ruby Beets Antiques,
Poxybogue Rd, Bridgehampton, Long Island, New York, USA
Painted furtiture, old white china and kitchenware.

Brimfield Market,
Massachusetts, USA
Held the first week of May, July and September; thousands of dealers and great antique buys.

The Conran Shop, 117 Rue du Bac, 75007 Paris, France
Contemporary furniture like its English counterpart.

Crate & Barrel, 650 Madison Avenue, New York, NY 10022, USA P.O. Box, 9059, Wheeling, Illinois 60090–9059, USA
www.crateandbarrel.com
A wonderful source of good value furniture and accessories, from simple white clean china and glass to chairs and beds.

English Country Antiques,
Snakehollow Road, Bridghampton, Long Island, NY 11932, USA
www.ecantiques.com
Period country furniture in pine, plus decorative blue-and-white china.

Habitat, Wagram, 35 Avenue de Wagram, 75017 Paris, France
www.habitat.co.uk
Stylish furniture and home basics.

Colette Aboudaram, Manpenti, 83136 La Roquebrussane Var, France
Decorative country furniture and antiques.

Hold Everything, P.O. Box 7807, San Francisco, CA 94120, USA (mail order)
Everything to do with storage from linen baskets to canvas shoe holders.

Ikea, 101 Rue Pereire, F78105, St. Germaine-en-les-Layes, France
www.ikea.co.uk
For home basics at great prices, including flatpack furniture and cheap stylish kitchenware.

Mombasa Net Canopies, 2345 Fort Worth St, Grand Prairie, Texas 75050, USA
Mosquito nets to make romantic bedhangings.

Benjamin Moore Paints, Montvale, New Jersey, New York, NY, USA
www.benjaminmoore.com
Good period style colours in muted shades.

Gladys Mougin, 30 Rue de Lille, Paris 75007, France
Tom Dixon lighting and other work by contemporary designers.

Palecek, P.O. Box 225, Station A, Richmond, CA 94808, USA
www.palecek.com
Wicker painted furniture.

Pottery Barn, 600 Broadway, New York NY 10012
P.O. Box 7044, San Francisco, CA 94120-7044 (mail order)
www.potterybarn.com
Everything from furniture to decorating details, such as muslin curtains, china, cushions and candlesticks.

Rose Brand Textiles, 517 West 35th St, New York, USA
www.rosebrand.com
Great value muslin, canvas, scrim and ticking.

Sage Street Antiques, Sag Harbour, Long Island, USA
Decorative period furniture and tableware.

Siècle, Rue du Bac 75005, Paris, France
Embroidered linens, cutlery and glass.

Takashimaya, 693 Fifth Avenue, New York, NY 10012, USA
Exquisite bedlinen, soaps and lotions.

Wolfman Gold & Good Co., 117 Mercer St, New York, NY 10012, USA

Jane Cumberbatch's best value top twenty

J.W. Bollom, 15 Theobalds Rd, London WC1X 8SN
www.bollom.com
Good paints and a huge variety of coloured felts.

Z. Butt Textiles, 248 Brick Lane, London E1
Denim, silk, calico, fabulous white cotton drill, muslin (all cheaper per metre if you buy at least l0 metres).

Habitat, I96 Tottenham Court Rd, London W1T 7LG
www.habitat.co.uk
Good cheap check fabric by the metre, kitchenware, cotton sheets and colourful bed throws; checked and striped cotton rugs.

Homebase, Beddington House, Wallington, Surrey FN6 OHB (branches around the country)
Flower pots, dustbins, kitchenware, storage boxes and other home basics.

Ikea, 2 Drury Way, North Circular Rd, London NW10 0TH
www.ikea.co.uk

Basic wooden tables and chairs, white fold-up cricket chairs; also good value sofas, kitchen units, cupboards and work surfaces; cheap glass tumblers; boxed sets of plain white china; tough Swedish-style cotton checked fabric.

Lakeland Plastics, Alexandra Buildings, Windermere, Cumbria LA23 1BQ (mail order)
Incredible selection of kitchen accessories, from string bags to plastic containers.

John Lewis, 278–306 Oxford St, London W1A 1EX
www.johnlewis.com
Brilliant kitchen and hardware department plus fabric, wool blankets, pillows, cushion pads, bolster pads, bath towels and sisal mats.

MacCulloch & Wallis, 25–26 Dering St, London W1R 0BH
www.macculloch-wallis.co.uk
Calico, muslin, gingham and a wide selection of haberdashery.

Ian Mankin, 109 Regent's Park Rd, London NW1 8UR
Great for cotton checks and stripes, always has some on sale at great discounts.

Pongees, 28–30 Hoxton Square, London N1 6NN
Silk specialists: a wide variety of weights, plus beautiful coloured parachute silks.

Price's Candles, 100 York Rd, London SW11 3RU
www.prices-candles.co.uk
A candle factory with just about every type of candle you could imagine; the creamy coloured ones are the best.

Russell & Chapple, 68 Drury Lane, London WC2B 5SP

Cotton, linen and my favourite green tent canvas.

Staines Catering Equipment, 15–19 Brewer St, London W1
White catering china (mugs, plates, soup, bowls), giant colanders, saucepans and pasta pots.

Woolworths,
www.woolworths.co.uk (branches around the country)
Good for kitchenware and bright plastic picnic ware.

Labocs & Wait, 18 Cheshire St, London E2
Great utility hardware and enamelled saucepans.

Paperchase, 213 Tottenham Court Rd, London W1T 9PS
www.paperchase.co.uk
Huge range of paper and art materials.

Anta, Fearn, Tan, Ross-shire, Scotland
The best and most robust woollen rugs, for picnics and the home.

V.V. Rouleaux, 54 Sloane Sq, SW1 8AW and 6 Marylebone High St, London W1M 3PB
www.vvrouleaux.com
Ribbons, cotton, velvet in bright greens and pinks – very stylish.

Robert Welch Designs, Lower High St, Chipping Camden, Gloucestershire GL55 6DY
Classic, simple cutlery – my favourite.

Waterford Wedgewood, 158 Regent St, London W1
Simple white dinner plates.

index